GRATOONY
THE
LOONY

THE WILD, UNPREDICTABLE
LIFE OF
GILLES GRATTON

BY GILLES GRATTON
AND GREG OLIVER

Published by ECW Press
665 Gerrard Street East
Toronto, Ontario, Canada M4M 1Y2
416-694-3348 / info@ecwpress.com

To the best of their abilities, the authors has related experiences, places, people, and organizations from their memories of them. In order to protect the privacy of others, they have, in some instances, changed the names of certain people and details of events and places.

LIBRARY AND ARCHIVES CANADA
CATALOGUING IN PUBLICATION

Gratton, Gilles, author
Gratoony the loony : the wild, unpredictable life of Gilles Gratton / Gilles Gratton and Greg Oliver.

ISSUED IN PRINT AND ELECTRONIC FORMATS.
ISBN 978-1-77041-337-5 (softcover)
978-1-77305-067-6 (PDF)
978-1-77305-068-3 (EPUB)

1. Gratton, Gilles. 2. Hockey goalkeepers—Canada—Biography. 3. Hockey players—Canada—Biography.
1. Oliver, Greg, author II. TITLE.

GV848.5.G69A3 2017   796.962092
C2017-902405-1   C2017-902984-3

Editor for the press: Michael Holmes
Cover design: David Gee
Cover Photo: © Bruce Jessop
Unless otherwise noted, photos are from the personal collection of Gilles Gratton.

The publication of *Gratoony the Loony* has been generously supported by the Government of Canada through the Canada Book Fund. *Ce livre est financé en partie par le gouvernement du Canada.* We also acknowledge the contribution of the Government of Ontario through the Ontario Book Publishing Tax Credit and the Ontario Media Development Corporation.

PRINTED AND BOUND IN CANADA

PRINTING: NORECOB   5   4   3   2   1

GRATOONY

THE

LOONY

THE WILD, UNPREDICTABLE
LIFE OF
GILLES GRATTON

For our children—Karine, Charlotte
and William Gratton, and Quinn Oliver.

"Religion is what prevents humanity from reaching a higher level of consciousness."

—Gilles Gurudas Losang Dawa Jarda Gratton

A LION IN WINTER

A great place to start is near the end—not with a spectacular save, a naked spin around the ice, or the tale of my past life as a solider in the Spanish Inquisition, but with a mask. Not just any mask either, but one of the most famous in hockey history.

My lion mask, vicious and snarling, dark and dangerous, debuted on January 30, 1977, at Madison Square Garden in New York City. It has come to define me, because most of the rest of my career was just a series of fuck-ups.

GREG HARRISON, MASKMAKER: He got more publicity from that mask than he ever did for any of his playing.

Goalies had worn masks regularly since Jacques Plante defied management and put his over his busted-up face in 1959. I was no different. But masks had no style, no personality. In junior hockey, with the Oshawa Generals, I had a really shitty brownish mask; well, it was shitty-looking, but it fit well and protected my face. In the WHA and then the NHL, I tried out a lot of different masks. There were form-fitting fibreglass masks and bulky cages where the bars bothered my eyes. With the New York Rangers, I once wore a different mask each period, but I still wasn't happy. Finally, I called up Greg Harrison.

He'd introduced himself earlier in the season as a maskmaker, something relatively new in our business. Harrison, who lived in Toronto, had painted masks for the likes of Jim Rutherford and Doug Favell. He was a beer-league goalie himself, and had graduated from art school, so he was an interesting cat with some pretty revolutionary ideas.

We met up at his home and he pitched a couple of ideas to me. We settled on a lion, since my astrological sign is Leo, and I'd found a great photo in a *National Geographic* magazine. He made an imprint of my face, and I left, waiting for the finished product.

GREG HARRISON: I had various pictures of lions, different angles, different shots, both at ease and snarling, and that's what I based it on. It wasn't airbrushed. It was done like an oil painting. The mask was finished on a Friday night. I painted it the next day. Then I baked it for a couple of hours in the oven to dry it, and put it into a box, took it to the airport. It went on a cheap seat on the plane, and off to New York. That was on the

Saturday. On the Sunday, he wore it. And the next day, it was all over the press. The following week, it was in *Time* magazine—it was on the same page as a picture of the Queen.

Greg wasn't there for the unveiling, which I played to the hilt.

MIKE McEWEN, RANGERS TEAMMATE AND ROOMMATE: I'm sitting at the dining room table, we're having dinner with my two sisters; they'd come down to visit. We hear the back door open up, the entrance to the kitchen, and he comes in and he's got the mask on. He runs into the dining room, right at the table, and growls like he's a lion. We look and go, "Ooooh." We were the first ones to see it.

We played St. Louis that night. When we got to Madison Square Garden, I had it in a box, under my dressing room stall. Nobody saw it. I warmed up with my cage mask. When I skated on the ice, I had the mask underneath my arm. It wasn't until they were about to start the game that I put my mask on. The crowd went Ooooh! The referees didn't start the game—they all came down to see my mask, referees and players. It was neat. We won the game 5–2, by the way, and it might have been the best $300 I ever spent.

My mask was a hit, and newspapers and TV stations in each city wanted to talk to me about it. Truthfully, it was one of the few highlights of that season with the Rangers. I fell out of favour with coach/GM John Ferguson, and was gone by the next year. I was so eager to get out of there that I left my equipment behind—including my mask. Harrison got it from Ferguson and then it went to the Hockey Hall of Fame. But I believe someone else owns it now.

Since then, it's appeared in books, on hockey cards and even on beer cans—the Molson Bubba mini-kegs as a part of its "The Art of Hockey" limited-edition run. The mask is better known than I ever was, which is somewhat appropriate. But for all its fame, it sure didn't have as much fun as I did . . .

So consider this fair warning before you read much further. My story doesn't follow the usual narrative for hockey sagas. While I had supportive parents who drove me to early morning games and worked extra shifts for me to get the equipment I needed, they were emotionally absent, meaning I grew up basically lawless and without discipline.

That carried over to my hockey career, and is much of the basis of my legend. I lived life to its fullest, even if I never bought into a life in hockey. There's a reason I walked away after my first full season in the National Hockey League. Actually, there are plenty of reasons, all of which you will hear about.

I'll tell funny stories, sure, but I also want people to understand me a little bit better by the end. I didn't want to play hockey, it just seemed that destiny pushed me into it.

They called me Gratoony the Loony, and truthfully, I never cared. A name's only a name, even if it was accurate. Anyway, that was just the press anyway.

You're in the public eye. You get insulting letters from people. You get booed. You get torn apart in the papers. And at some point, you just stop caring. When people said things about me, it was water off a duck's back. I didn't get insulted. Now, if it's in person at an autograph signing, and they start insulting me to

See how fierce I look in my mask! *International Hockey Archives*

my face, there's a problem. But what I've come to realize is that if someone is a prick with me, he's probably a prick with just about everyone, because that's his inner state. I can't take that personally, since I don't know what drove him to be an asshole—maybe his wife just left him, or he owes a lot of money. I never take things personally.

In the end, they can't see the real me anyway. All they see is my body.

Growing up, my friends called me Joe; damned if I know why, though Gilles always sounded feminine to me. On the Toronto Toros, it was Cookie—because I do a great impression of the Cookie Monster from *Sesame Street*—or Gilley. My teammates with the Rangers called me Count. Now, at work, they call me Pooch, Poochilina, or Poochie, all in reference to the queen of blow jobs in Cherry Hill, New Jersey . . . I'll tell you about that later.

You're going to read about some of the usual hockey shit, of course, but I'm going to tell you the real stories—the sex, the drugs, the booze, the lonely nights, the wacky owners and clueless coaches . . . and my own personal search for the meaning of it all.

Some of the names have had to be changed or omitted to protect the not-so-innocent. There are plenty of reasons why. Kudos to those who have stepped forward and offered up their own recollections of those days to help tell my story—it's not like I remember it all.

In fact, I'm still looking for my shirt from that New York Rangers booster party in late 1976.

CHAPTER 1

GROWING UP

A line from the movie *The Accidental Tourist* has stuck with me through the years, and it perfectly sums up my childhood. William Hurt is talking to his wife, Kathleen Turner, not long after their son died, and he says, "I endure. I'm holding steady." That was me. In French, it's *malaise de vivre*, a sickness or trauma over living.

Some would probably label it depression, but it wasn't exactly that. Another way I might say it in French would be *mal-être*, which could translate as continual unease in being alive, or *angoisse existentielle*, which means existential angst.

My childhood was very difficult because of all the questions I had. I was very surprised to end up in this body. What am I doing on this planet? I especially had a hard time pretending things were important, and still do. You win the Stanley Cup, but what does it mean? People skate around, they kiss the Cup. What does that mean? It means fuck all. It's insignificant, just like the fact that there are more stars in the heavens than grains of sand on a beach. In the grand scheme of things, being a good person, treating your wife and kids and other people well, means far more than winning the Stanley Cup.

When I was a kid, that was my main frame of thought. "What am I doing here? Why did I end up in this body?" I was in utter anguish, and would wake up in the middle of the night and just sit at the kitchen table for hours, thinking.

I never did talk to anyone about the way I was feeling, because I didn't want anybody else to feel like I did. I thought that if I told them the way I felt about life, the universe, how lost I was, it might affect them and make them feel the same way. That's why I kept it to myself. I certainly never talked to my parents about it, because I didn't think they would understand. These were very deep, existential thoughts. Today, there is a lot more help available—people to talk to—but when I was growing up, there wasn't.

The best way for me to get away from the suffering was to participate in sports. In the winter, I would skate from morning to night, only taking breaks for meals. The city rink was right in front of my house. I wouldn't even take my skates off when I came in the house. I'd sit on the stairs still wearing them, eat, and then head back. At dinner time, I'd take them off, rub my feet for a while before dinner, and head back out.

My goal was to exhaust myself. In the summer, it was tennis or baseball, and I would play all day. If there was no one to play with, I'd throw a ball against a wall for hours. Physically, if I was exhausted, I could find peace; with my brain too worn out to dwell on my thoughts, I could sleep.

It was really hard to go through life and pretend that I cared. If we played hockey or baseball, and we won, I had to act happy. But I wasn't. I was indifferent. It made no difference. What difference does it make when you're 11 years old and you hit a home run to win a game? What difference does it make when everyone dies?

I've struggled for years trying to figure out where all these thoughts came from, but have never found a satisfactory answer.

My parents, Fernand and Thérèse, were raised on farms in the Ottawa Valley about a mile apart, on RR 18 between

Me with my brothers Jacques and Norm in 1958. *Courtesy Chantal Puyleart*

Casselman and Saint-Isidore, about an hour's drive from Ottawa itself. My dad never went to school. All he knew was working, whether on the farm or later at Standard Brands in Montreal, where he was a machinist.

The five Gratton kids were all born in Montreal. There's Jacques, born in 1949; Norm in 1950; me, born July 28, 1952; Claudine, born in 1956; and François, born in 1960.

Despite my angst, I do have some fond memories of growing up. In particular, we used to visit my grandparents almost every weekend until hockey started taking over. Our holidays were in the Ottawa Valley too—we never took a vacation anywhere else. My grandparents on my mother's side were named Castonguay. My grandparents on my father's side lived one farm over from my Castonguay grandparents. I never liked going to my Gratton grandparents when I was little, and as soon as we got out of the car me and my brothers Jacques and Norm would run over to our Castonguay grandparents a mile down the road. They were just wonderful grandparents.

In the summer we loved spending time on their farm. I was too young to help much, but I can remember my brothers doing chores around the farm. I would often sit on my grandfather's lap while he drove the tractor. He would be driving, but I'd have my hands on the wheel. We'd be pulling a wagon, and my father and my uncles would be tossing hay onto the tractor. It was a big family; I got to spend time with my uncles, aunts and cousins.

We lived in a part of Montreal known as LaSalle, in a house my father built in 1948 with the help of my two grandfathers and my uncles; I think it cost him $5,000, money that he borrowed from the bank. More specifically, we lived in an area called the Highlands, where four streets near the train tracks—Highlands, Stirling, Strathyre and Riverview—made for their own enclave. And even then it was split: Avenue Highlands had mostly French-speaking families, Strathyre and Riverview had mostly English, and Stirling was a mix. French was pretty well the language in the area, though. The other side of the tracks was another world. We never played with them, though there were times we crossed the tracks to play sports against them.

FRANÇOIS GRATTON: You could go out of the house in LaSalle, and there were plenty of kids. Everybody was playing outside. There was no colour TV, no technology. Everybody was playing baseball, football and hockey outside. It was full of kids. No one was well educated. Our town was not a high-class town. Everybody was rough.

There were big families all around, and ours was actually small in comparison. There were families with eight, nine, a dozen kids. Sometimes when we played baseball in front of the house, it could be 15 against 15. It was a safe, working-class neighbourhood. The mothers were all home, and we'd go home at all times of the day. Hand-me-down clothes were normal, and no one had extra money for extravagances.

My sense of humour developed and showed itself early. Usually in French Canada you get your middle name from your godfather. My brother Norm was Normand Lionel Joseph Gratton, because my uncle Lionel was his godfather. My paternal grandfather, Ben Gratton, was my godfather. But his real name was Bélani. When I first went to school, the teacher asked what our full names were. I thought my name was Joseph Gilles Baloney Gratton, so that's what I told the teacher. She put me in the corner to punish me because she thought I was making fun of her. She called my mom, and said, "Your son is a little bastard because he's only six years old and he's starting to make people laugh." My mom told her that my grandfather's name was Bélani. The teacher apologized to my mom and then things were okay. When your school days start like that, you know you're going to have a weird life. My actual given name is Joseph Jean Gilles Gratton, in case you're wondering. As for the teacher, I saw her in the park just a few years ago, and she still loves to tell the "baloney" story.

When I was about eight years old, I worked at a depanneur, a small grocery store. Claude Bertrand had been my best friend since about the age of five, and it was his uncle's store, and we worked side by side. Claude's uncle gave us a dollar an hour to do all kinds of jobs. We'd help unload, sort things in the basement. It was my money to do what I wanted with, and it felt like a fortune. It was my mom who kept the finances in the house. In fact, I don't even think my father knew how much he made on his paycheque. He was a very quiet man. He would come home on the Thursday and hand his cheque to my mother.

Unlike most other French-Canadian families, our parents were not religious. They went to church but never pushed us into any of that. I think my mom went to make friends who she could play cards with—she loved to play cards and socialize, which was the opposite of my father. She loved to laugh and often gleefully told stories about whatever dumb thing her boys had done at school.

Unlike my dad, she was able to show emotion, but our family was not like others. On birthdays, no one really said anything, no one wished you happy birthday, and there certainly weren't presents. When dad got angry, he could be intimidating, but never violent.

DAN BOUCHARD, CHILDHOOD FRIEND AND FUTURE NHL GOALIE: Mr. Gratton was a hardworking man, a very funny man. He had restraint. He would never swear. His favourite saying was *régiboire*, which was just some kind of a slang, not a cuss word.

6

We just did our own thing and found out about the world on our own. And because my dad worked shifts, he never seemed to be home. You can tell by the life I had—I screwed up so many times—that I didn't have any direction.

Here's a good example. There was a monastery on the other side of the tracks with an apple orchard. It was great fun sneaking in there to steal apples, but then we didn't eat them; instead, we'd throw them at passing buses. Early in the summer when I was nine, though, I fell out of a tree in the orchard. The impact broke my elbow, leaving everything below the joint just hanging there. Doctors had to reconstruct my elbow in three separate operations. It took about a year to heal, and then I had to get the movement back. My two brothers and I slept in the same room, and in the morning when I got up, I would wake them with the cracks of my elbow.

There was a definite lack of respect for authority on the part of me and my friends. I had a buddy Garry McDermid—funny name for a French guy, eh?—and we used to play baseball as teenagers. After a game, we'd climb the lights and, hanging on precariously, take a shit down, listening for the satisfying splat. Or we would go down to the river and grab an eel from the St. Lawrence, and when the bus came by, we'd throw the eel on people in the bus.

Since so few people had cars, we took the bus a lot. I do wonder if the bus drivers had photos of us up at their station. We used to piss on the floor of the bus, especially later at night. Another time, coming back from Montreal—LaSalle was the last stop on the route—we'd been really loud. At the last stop, the driver came down the aisle and told us to get out. We got off the bus but the driver was still giving me shit: "If I was your dad, I'd kick your ass."

Garry went up behind him and kicked him in the ass. That allowed me to take off, and Garry wasn't far behind. The driver chased us for a bit, but we picked up some stones and started throwing them at the bus. He then got back in and drove away.

It was the same in school. There were many teachers I told off. In the third grade, I started going off the rails a bit. Almost every day, I'd have to stay late to copy out 300 lines of "I won't do this or that . . ."

Not all of the gang was like me. My buddy from the store, Claude, was level-headed, which resulted in a 35-year career as a landscape architect. When we were six, we were out on the tracks in front of our house in the winter, and we found a bottle on the track with liquid in it. I said to Claude, "We should drink it." He said no way. He was not the adventurous one. I put the bottle to my nose to smell it, and my nose started to burn—it was acid. I had a hole in my nose for years, and there's still a mark there. He saved my life, because I was going to drink it.

Even when it was something as important to me as hockey at the rink across the street, I couldn't resist being a little shit. The rink was lit up until 10 at night, and after that, the man who ran the rink, Mr. Kostik, would go out to flood it. Me and my buddies would goof around with his hose, and often he'd run after us. We'd have the hose pinched so it wasn't working on his end, and when he got near us, we'd let it go and it would spray everywhere. But then after a while, we started helping him, shovelling the rink and helping to flood the ice.

During the summer, baseball was the game. There wasn't a proper diamond in the park, but that didn't matter. Kids would just come and go during the game, and it just seemed to run all day. We didn't need adults organizing us. I actually got pretty good, mainly playing left field. The Montreal Expos once called to invite me to a camp, but I had committed to hockey by that point.

There have been many moments through the years where I have wondered about the different paths my life could have taken. I am most curious about what could have happened had I followed my love of music.

I was 12 when Beatlemania struck. Me and my buddies all bought guitars, and we played Beatles, Beatles, Beatles. I never took lessons; we learned from each other. We had some books that had the chords. Then you'd learn a riff from one guy, and then something else from someone else. I had a really good ear for music, and could play just about anything having just heard the song.

> **CLAUDE BERTRAND:** We jumped into
> Beatlemania. The British Invasion hit LaSalle,
> on Montreal's west side, but in the east side it
> was more French, with French artists. We learned
> English from the Beatles. We did not really
> understand the words that we were singing, we
> didn't understand the lyrics.

We were obsessed. The only albums I'd buy were by the Beatles. I had my hair cut like the Beatles. At first, John Lennon was my favourite, but then it became George Harrison—especially when the Beatles broke up. I thought John's energy with Yoko wasn't any good. As for Paul McCartney, I thought his music was just garbage. The Beatles did play in Montreal, but I was too young to go.

My parents weren't musical, so I don't know where my brother Jacques and I got our talent. He was a tenor and took music lessons, which meant my parents bought a piano when I was a teenager so Jacques could practice his scales. I can still hear his booming voice filling up the house, and I learned the songs of French crooners like Charles Aznavour and Gilbert Bécaud. Next thing you know, I sat down and just started playing the piano. It was second nature. Again, I never took a lesson. Like with the guitar, if I heard something, I could play it.

We were a real garage band, and one summer we teamed up to move the piano to the garage, too. My mom would come out when she'd had enough and threaten to turn off the electricity. The cops used to come around at one in the morning and tell us to settle down a bit, because the neighbours were complaining. We'd stop for a bit and then we'd start again. When they came the second time, we'd stop for good. We did a few of our own songs, but mainly it was covers of Beatles songs. We got only a handful of gigs, including at my sister's wedding.

Through the years, I continued to play music with my buddies, just hanging out and shooting the shit. On the road, I might have my guitar with me, or sit down at a piano in the hotel lobby. I even recorded a few things, though I know I have a terrible voice. One of the songs I recorded was called "Symbiotic Angel." I did it in the late 1990s with my friend Claude. I'm way better at the music than I am with the vocals.

Jacques also learned about astrology from his music teacher. It's a funny thing—she was teaching him singing and astrology. I learned from him and read all his books. It just grew from there, and I started reading about astrology, meditation and the occult. I found that as I got into it, I could guess people's astrological signs just from the way they behaved or the way they talked, and sometimes even from their physical appearance. It's usually quite easy.

So here I was, a decided oddball right from the start, with a fascination with subjects that most people never get into, let alone as a kid. Instead of pursuing the freewheeling lifestyle of a musician, I went into the established, traditional world of minor hockey, never thinking there would be the possibility of one day playing in the National Hockey League.

CHAPTER 2

PUT THE LITTLE KID IN NET

For many years, youth hockey in Quebec was dominated by the Church. The local parish had equipment to suit up kids for games against other parishes. You usually just had to provide your own skates. It was no different in LaSalle, except all of the equipment was based at our school, not at the church. It was almost a community centre set up, with Ping-Pong tables and other indoor activities designed to keep kids from getting into mischief. The rink was across the street from my house, and it would be in place by mid-November and last until March.

If I wanted to play at the peewee level, though, I had to play with boys bigger than me, including my brother Norm, who was two years older. The church's goalie was Dan Bouchard, who

Three NHL players are in this photo: Dan Bouchard is holding
the bats in the middle; to his right-hand side is my brother Norm;
I'm in the second row, far right with dirty blond hair.

would go on to have a lengthy NHL career. But at the time, the
coaches decided that Dan needed the challenge of bantam-level
hockey rather than staying in peewee, and that decision would
change my life.

When a team needs a goalie, what do they do? They take the
smallest guy, which was me, and they put him in net. Up until
that point, I'd been a forward, like Norm.

I thought I'd try it just for fun—and fun it was. It was also
a good feeling to be relied upon by your teammates. When I

Not a Beatles haircut at all, eh?
Courtesy Claude Bertrand

played goal, I didn't have a clue. There was no hockey school, no one taught me. I just played. Our coaches were parents, volunteers. They didn't know much.

We took our bath on Saturday night, and then we'd sit in front of the television for the second period of the game on *La Soirée du hockey* on Radio-Canada. I followed NHL hockey until I was about 12 years old, and then I drifted away and didn't watch as often. I didn't have any goaltending role models to help me along the way.

But somehow I did okay, and was even chosen to be a part of a team of the best players made up from our church league in LaSalle to go to Quebec City and play in the massive peewee tournament there. It was quite the experience, with teams from all over. We didn't do especially well, but it was a taste of a higher level of hockey.

Another taste came courtesy Jacques Lemaire. His family lived four streets from my place, on the same street as the school, where his brother was in my class. Jacques was playing for the Lachine Maroons in the Metropolitan Junior League, and we'd walk along 19th Avenue to see him play on Sundays. It cost 10 cents to get into the game. On Saturday mornings he would go to the rink in front

Hanging out with my buddies in the spring of 1969.
Courtesy Claude Bertrand

of my house and he would practice slapshots. At least once, I went in net for him. I don't even know if he knows that was me. He'd be at the blue line practicing. He was careful because he was a junior and I was just peewee, so he would shoot low on me, not high.

The next level for me was bantam, and I actually played on two teams for a season. I played forward for my parish, but when I played for LaSalle, I played goal. In my second year of bantam, I only played goal, for LaSalle. We had a great team, and we won the All-Quebec championships.

I only played one year of midget hockey. Most of my bantam teammates had moved up together to midget, and we won the

All-Quebec championship again. I wasn't the reason we won—our best player was Serge Martel—but in 77 midget games, I had a 1.06 goals against average. That got me onto the radar for the next level, Junior B, though it didn't hurt that Norm had started playing with the Montreal Junior Canadiens.

I only played eight games for LaSalle in Junior B. The details are fuzzy—I suffered two concussions early that season.

> **CLAUDINE CLOUTIER-GRATTON:** He had a slapshot right in the head. He fell down and we were looking at him. We went under the stands, because he had to go by ambulance to the hospital. He was knocked out. When he opened his eyes, my mother looked at him and said, "Gilles, Gilles, how do you feel?" He looked at her and said, "I think a bee just hit me."

I ended up spending six days in the hospital, and it wasn't until the fourth day that I could even sit up in bed. When I finally did leave, it was in a wheelchair, and then to bed at home for another week. Fortunately, I was still able to read, and I was fascinated by books on reincarnation, Tibetan Buddhism, and many other subjects that preteens aren't usually into. My idol was the Dalai Lama, not Maurice Richard.

When I did go back in net, in March, I got hit in the back of the head with a stick. When I went back to the dressing room, I started to throw up and I could hardly stand on my feet. After another three days in bed at home from that second concussion, I told my parents I was not going to play hockey ever again. I didn't give a shit. Life happens. I considered what to do next. I hated school, so I didn't plan on continuing; college would have been more of the same. It's likely I would have drifted into music full time had it not been for Chuck Catto.

He was a scout for the Boston Bruins and came by our home in the summer of 1969. I can still remember his pitch: "I followed you in bantam and midget, and saw you win All-Quebec, and I have faith in you. I can put my reputation on the line by giving you a contract in Oshawa." He was offering me not a tryout but a contract. My parents really didn't make a big deal of it. My mom said, "Do you want to go?" It's not like today, with kids being scouted from an early age and dealing with agents. It was a different era.

I turned 17 that summer, and since I didn't know what to do with my life, I thought, "Well, let's try this. If it doesn't work out, I'll just come back." I figured I'd at least learn some English.

This is where Dan Bouchard made every difference. Physically, I wasn't feeling very well; I still had headaches almost every day, starting in the morning, followed by dizzy spells later in the day. I thought I was in way over my head going to Oshawa, because I felt so weak. But Dan trained with me and encouraged me. He got me in shape. He was such a positive guy, so it grew on me that maybe I could do it. Dan had been playing net in Sorel with the QMJHL Black Hawks, and he'd learned muscle-stretching exercises from his sister, Sylvia, who was a figure skater.

For weeks that summer, we worked on improving my balance and my ability to move backwards quickly. To improve our glove hands, we'd either throw or hit lacrosse balls back and forth at each other, which flew back far faster than tennis balls. But as much as it was about reflexes and sharpening skills, it was also just a couple of buddies hanging out, shooting the shit while we threw lacrosse balls against the wall.

DAN BOUCHARD: We had a lot of fun. We were just normal kids. But he was always asking me, "Why are you doing this? Why are you doing that?" He was always trying to get to the bottom of things. Then, after your career, you know a little bit more, but I would teach him the neuro-muscular stuff, how the brain works—I did not know I was teaching him that, but that's what I was doing. "When the ball comes off the wall, you've got to pick it up, and in the next move, you've got to see it go in your glove. That's your timing, the gap time."

As the summer ended, my dad drove me to the train station in Montreal for the trip to Oshawa. There wasn't going to be anything emotional coming from him. Just: "See you later."

CHAPTER 3

GENERAL GRATTON

I felt like an impostor when I got to Oshawa. I had just turned 17 and was skinny as shit, 5-foot-11 and about 150 pounds. I found myself in the training camp for the Oshawa Generals—and I barely spoke any English. I hadn't even played hockey the year before, and there I was, with a contract. There's 12 goalies in camp and I'm already on the team. I remember thinking, "Shit, this isn't right . . ." I didn't feel I deserved to be there. To complicate things, since I was in the Ontario league, they had to get clearance from the Quebec league for me to even play—though I had played in a couple of exhibition games. My permission finally came on October 6, a handful of games into the season. Ted McComb was the other goalie, so he started the games early in the season, with Bryan Rose backing him up.

My brother Jacques sang the national anthem when he was in Oshawa.
Photo by Bill Stewart,
courtesy Wayne Kewin

Believe it or not, in my first game, we beat the Toronto Marlies 6–3 and I stopped 38 shots. During one 30-second span in the second period, I made stops on Steve Shutt, Mike Murphy and John French. I got first star, and got to do a little wave to the crowd at our home rink, the Civic Auditorium. It was also my introduction to the rivalry between the Marlies and Generals, two teams only about 45 minutes apart. There was something deeper rooted too, with Oshawa being such a working-class town, reliant on General Motors and the auto industry for work, while Toronto was the bustling big city, the provincial capital.

Our team had six kids who were raised in the area too—Ted McComb, Bryan Rose, Hank Nowak, Terry O'Reilly, Tom Simpson, Terry Rowland—and they always got pumped for playing Toronto.

TED McCOMB, GENERALS GOALTENDER: If you were an Oshawa kid, you had to be almost head

and shoulders better than anybody else, because
they seemed to prefer bringing in people than
giving an Oshawa kid a chance. It just so happened
that year, Henry and myself and Terry O'Reilly,
we had played on an All-Ontario championship
midget team, so you're not going to get better
hockey players than on a team that wins an Ontario
championship. They could have actually picked
up a few more guys, but they didn't. There were a
couple of guys from Whitby on the team too.

In another game early in the season, we got pummelled 8–1 by
the Montreal Junior Canadiens. McComb started the game, and
I came in at the start of the third period, already down 6–1. My
brother Norm had scored goals four, five and six for the Baby Habs,
and his fourth goal of the game came against me in the first shot of
the third. I settled down from there, but we were clearly outclassed.

Between me and McComb, it looked like the Generals had
two decent 17-year-old goalies. It was odd seeing my photo in
the *Oshawa Times* newspaper, and even odder seeing nice things
written about me. Here's a few lines from a column by George H.
Campbell, who was the associate sports editor:

> *Gilles Gratton, Oshawa's new French-Canadian
> goalie, made a hit with the fans. The flamboyant type,
> with plenty of confidence, he showed he's already learned
> quite a few tricks about this puck-stopping business. His
> work in the first two periods especially was just great.
> Colorful, with that flair that will make a hit with the
> home fans and probably irk the opposition, there was*

no mistaking his own sheer satisfaction and pleasure in the win. His enthusiasm in acknowledging his choice as one of the game's Three Stars indicated that. The combination of Gilles and "Steady Teddy" could be just the answer for the Generals' goalkeeping chores.

Since my English wasn't great, when I talked to the press I always stuck to the line that I needed to see a lot of shots in a game to feel sharp. That wasn't bullshit either—it was really the way I felt. If you get bored from the lack of action, then you are prone to stupid mistakes. Given the youth of our team, facing shots was never an issue.

I only went to high school for a couple of days in Oshawa, which I sort of regret now, but at the time I was in way over my head. I was standing there, and they were calling names for roll call. When the name Gilles *Graa-ton* was called—said in an Anglicized way, with a long a—I didn't answer. By the end of the roll call, I was the only guy left. The teacher turned to me and said, "What's your name?" I said, "Gilles Gratton." He looked back at the list and sent me to class. I lasted three days.

Despite the lack of formal education, my English came along quickly, and it helped that so many hockey terms were interchangeable in either language. My protector was "Hound Dog" Bob Kelly, who'd go on to fame with the Broad Street Bully Philadelphia Flyers. We roomed together at a boarding house arranged by the team, run by an older couple. I wasn't going to school, so I could sleep in. Every morning, he'd get up and put the Supremes on the stereo. I'd be in bed trying to sleep some more. His wardrobe was white T-shirts—he had maybe 10 of them. He wore really, really tight jeans. Pointy black shoes. He'd slick his blond hair back again and again in front of the mirror, like he was the Fonz. He had an old '64 Meteor that he loved to cruise around town in.

Since I wasn't in school, I had a couple of day jobs. My first year, I worked at a huge hardware store with a guy from Lancashire, England. For the first two weeks, I don't think I understood a word he said. He had a really strong accent. But he's the one who really helped me learn English. At first, I had a strange accent, but over time I changed it. In my second and third years in town, I worked at a TV shop on Simcoe Street. In the morning, I would watch *Sesame Street* until I was needed to help deliver a television. It was a really easy job. I just sat and watched TV.

The coach in Oshawa my first year was Doug Williams, and he didn't know piss all about hockey, even though he'd worked with Bobby Orr when he was a General. Apparently, he'd played senior hockey for the Whitby Dunlops, but they must have been desperate. He was the vice-principal of a secondary school in Oshawa, so he had two jobs—and big, bushy eyebrows. The GM was Matt Leyden, and the only things I remember about him are that he was really old and that he was the one who picked me up at the train station.

The *Oshawa Times* had a column where Coach Williams answered questions from fans. One that ran was about how Teddy and I differed in net, and it was actually relatively insightful:

> *Coach Doug Williams, when describing his netminders, refers to them as a unit, not individually. "Both are very aggressive," he stated recently. "They come out of the net to give our guys heck when it is needed and are talking it up all the time."*
> *"Both Gilles and Ted are really bearing down in*

practices these days. They are getting far more shooting because both of them want it and ask for it."

It seems strange that two players with much the same approach to the game, vary to such an extent in the personality department.

McComb, for example, a product of the Oshawa Minor System, is the quieter and more conservative of the two. He had a habit early in the season to taking his games home with him and replaying them over and over in his mind.

"People say I look cool on the ice," McComb said recently, "but really I'm quite nervous. I'm not getting down on myself after a bad game as much as I used to. I've come to realize that I must make goals scored on me good goals because the bad goals are the ones that get me down."

Gratton, the colorful French-Canadian from LaSalle, unlike McComb, tries to release his emotions in the dressing room and on the ice.

"I feel nervousness in me before a game," Gratton stated, "but I try to get rid of it by talking it out. If I don't, I just get tired physically and mentally."

"When I start a game I try to play a good first five minutes. I like to have one or two real hard stops, and I shout and shout at the other players. It gets me into the game."

Williams, commenting on the strong points of his two netminders, said, "Ted has an excellent glove hand. He will play the puck more often with the glove than will Gilles. In tight, though, Gilles is at his best

*because he is very accomplished with his stick. He likes
to poke check in the style of Johnny Bower."*

*One of the most difficult decisions a coach can
make is when to pull a goaltender during the course of
a bad game. Williams says all you can really do is go
by instinct.*

*"It is hard to choose the proper time because the
situation is much like pulling a pitcher in baseball. In
the back of your mind you keep thinking he will come
back. But I've reached the stage where I look at the
goalies as a forward line, or a defensive unit. If you have
the strength on the bench, you must make use of it."*

*Hockey goaltending is probably one of the most
difficult positions to play in any sport. The physical
and mental requirements at times are overwhelming.*

*Both netminders were asked if they enjoyed
their jobs. Gratton was the first to answer and,
surprisingly, he stated he didn't like goaltending itself,
but he enjoyed the challenge that it entailed.*

*"When you are in goal," he replied, "there are really
two teams that go on the ice. There are the forwards
and defencemen and then there are Ted and myself.
If they make a mistake it doesn't mean a goal, if we
make a mistake it does."*

*"Goaltending is a challenge because if I quit now
I'll consider myself a nobody. But if I get through
Junior A and into the NHL, then I'll know I've
accomplished something. I'll be proud of myself."*

*McComb in answering the question said, "After
I played a good game I think goal is the best position*

in the world. But when we lose I blame myself. I like catching things, and I like making big saves that can lift spirits up. If I didn't play goal I don't think I could have gone as far as I have in any other position."

I doubt that anyone noticed, or cared about, how I was feeling. And I still had the sense that I was an impostor, that I didn't belong, though I did get my head shaved in the rookie initiation; but even that didn't really matter to me—it was just a little colder in the rink. I called my parents and said, "I'm coming home at Christmas and I'm not going back." They said that was fine.

I took my suitcases back home, and didn't tell anyone in Oshawa. In my mind, I was going home and not going back. There were only 54 games in those days. I spent Christmas at my house, and my Dad says, "Well, what are you going to do?" I said, "I don't know, maybe go to work or something." He said, "There's only three months left. Why don't you go back and finish your year." He wasn't pushing me, but it made sense, so I returned.

My family came to see me play on occasion.

CLAUDINE CLOUTIER-GRATTON: When I was young, we would take the car on Sunday morning and would drive to Oshawa, where Gilles was playing in the afternoon, and sometimes Norm was playing in Toronto with the Junior Canadiens. So we would see Gilles in Oshawa, Norm in Toronto and come back overnight, arriving home at six o'clock in the morning. We did lots of travelling to Oshawa.

I can distinctly remember my brother Jacques coming to a game, and he sat in the corner with some of my friends. Jacques was a closeted homosexual at the time and had some eccentric friends. The Canadian national anthem began playing, and Jacques started to sing. You could hear him in the arena—and he had no microphone. His voice was that powerful. I'm standing in net, and I'm kind of embarrassed. Everybody turned to look at him. After that, every time he came to town over my three years in Oshawa, management got him to sing the anthem at centre ice. In retrospect, he would probably would not have gotten the same opportunity if everyone knew he was gay. Keeping in line with the closed nature of our family, we didn't know Jacques was gay until he was in his 40s. He had girlfriends as a teenager and was married and divorced by the time he came out.

One of the first games back after Christmas came against the London Knights, with my old buddy Dan Bouchard in net. (They won 7–2.) Dan had played with Sorel in the Quebec junior league, but like me, had gone east to Ontario.

The best team in the league, by a long margin, was the Montreal Junior Canadiens, with Gilbert Perreault as their star. They only lost two games in the Forum that season, and one of them was to me, 5–4. We played three games there. I tied them, beat them and lost, so three points out of six. It was an example of how much better I would play in Quebec, in front of friends and family, which was a pattern that would repeat throughout my brief time in the WHA and NHL.

That year, we would take the train to Montreal, play on a Sunday night, take the train back and be in Oshawa early on Monday morning. The sleeping berths were used for card games and drinking, not a good night's sleep. After that, we were forbidden from taking the train. We had to bus it in subsequent years.

When our coach wasn't Coach Williams, he was Vice-Principal Williams at O'Neill Collegiate, and his players/students knew it.

> **BOB KELLY, GENERALS LEFT WING:** We'd take the long train ride home from Montreal, and everybody who went to his school had to go to school when they got off the train at six o'clock in the morning. If we didn't go to his school, we'd just go home and go to bed.

Like all teenagers, we partied quite a bit too. That's how I started drinking—at parties, at 17. There would be team parties at someone's place, with the team and girls and friends. One time we had a party at a motel and the cops came, and we flew out the windows to escape. Every time I went to a party, Bob Kelly would ask me to play the guitar, and he always requested the Beatles song "You Really Got a Hold on Me." Then I'd do Neil Young's "Heart of Gold" and make the guys laugh by changing the lyrics from Hollywood to "H-Oshawa." And there was more innocent fun at the local pool.

> **NELSON PYATT, GENERALS CENTRE:** Typical Gilles. He'd be diving off the diving board and doing cannonballs, and would yank down his trunks. Everyone would laugh. He did everything for a laugh.

Our team started to come together as the season went on, and we strung together a couple of winning streaks. Since we didn't have a superstar like Perreault or Marcel Dionne of the St. Catharines Black Hawks, we had to rely on checking and forcing the other team into mistakes. The Generals finished 8th out of 10 teams (17 wins, 27 losses and 10 ties), and we were tied with the Hamilton Red Wings in the final standings with 44 points, a whopping 35 points back of Montreal. It was like neither team wanted to be there—we lost 4–2 to Toronto in our last game, and Hamilton fell to London 3–2. Defenceman Bob Stewart was our lone all-star.

We had a play-in game against the Wings at Maple Leaf Gardens, and I was in net. That was a weird game. We were winning 2–0 with four minutes to go, and Hamilton scored two goals to tie it. One was a wide shot that missed the net but took a wicked bounce off the backboards, right to centre Terry Ryan; I was out of position at the side of the net, going to play the puck. The second one was what they would call goaltender interference today—a Red Wing drove Bob Stewart into me at the side of the net, and the puck went to winger Ron Climie with a wide-open net. Then they scored two goals in the first five minutes of overtime—it was a 10-minute extra period. So they were leading 4–2, and then we tied it up. Our hero in overtime was Tom Simpson, who took a slapshot from a bad angle on the right side of the rink, and it went through a maze of players to beat goalie Mike Veisor.

We got 44 shots on Veisor, and I faced 41. The Oshawa newspaper said that I displayed "amazing coolness under fire," and asked me about it after. "I was nervous all the way through. I didn't get down, though, after their tying goal. I knew we could come back," I said.

It was a big deal that we made the playoffs in Oshawa. The team hadn't been there since 1966, when the Bobby Orr–led team made the Memorial Cup finals but didn't win. The newspaper proclaimed the "playoff famine" over.

Up next were the Toronto Marlies, and they were a much better team than us. The series was first to eight points, with two for a win, one for a tie. We went down in five games, only tying the second one. I played in a couple of the games, but we were just overmatched by the likes of Mike Murphy, who got five goals in the series, Dale Tallon, who had four, and Steve Shutt with three. It didn't help that our best scorer, Pete Sullivan, hurt his shoulder against Hamilton and couldn't go in this round.

My statistics weren't bad for a rookie: I played 28 games, winning 8, losing 15, and tying 3. I gave up 129 goals for a goals-against average of 4.96.

In the summer, it sure wasn't about working out and getting better like it is for the players today. I hung around the swimming pool with my buddies and played music. For exercise, mostly I played tennis or racquetball.

As for my second year in Oshawa, let's just say that my concentration wasn't there—and you can tell by my 4.99 average. That year, I had a girlfriend, Marion, who was later named Miss Oshawa. Hockey wasn't a focus. She was an usher. I was with her every day. I spent my whole year in love. After spending all my spare time with Marion, I'd go to bed at four or five in the morning (I lived with the Woodcock family, and "Woody" liked to drink, so I did too, more than usual) and get up in time for practice, after all the other guys were getting home from school. I honestly don't know why the Generals stuck with me, why they kept their faith in me. That second year in Oshawa, I was just terrible, and the team wasn't much better. We didn't even win until our tenth game, and finished out of the playoffs with an 18–37–7 record. In one game, we got destroyed 16–1 by the Marlies, and GM Matt Leyden credited me with "keeping the score down."

Junior hockey has always had its wild side—teenagers hopped up on adrenaline (and other things), wanting to impress. The one incident that has stuck with me came at the end of February, at Maple Leaf Gardens. The Marlies had a killer line of Steve Shutt, Billy Harris and Dave Gardner, and in that game, Shutt joined Gardner at 100 points in the season. As for Harris, he fractured his knuckle on my head early in the second period.

Playing at home in the Oshawa Civic Auditorium.

BILLY HARRIS, MARLIES RIGHT WING: He took a swing at me. I turned around and speared him—back then, they just used to wear the mask, no cages or anything—right up under the chin on the throat. I go into the corner to get the puck and the next thing I know, I've got two goalie gloves wrapped around me. He chased me in the corner

and jumped on my back. I flipped him off and hit
him in the side of the head behind the mask, and
I broke my hand hitting him in the head.

Steve Shutt was a danger every game. Our equipment was so
shitty and he had that big slapshot. I had so many bruises on my
shoulders and my arms. Another nightmare to play against was
Marcel Dionne, who was with St. Catharines in my final OHA
season. He was a shifty little player, and when he shot, he usually
came across the blueline, and *plouk!* He would just snap the wrist,
top corner. Marcel was a dangerous man on the ice, and was the
guy I had the hardest time against, probably in the pros too.

Then there was Gilbert Perreault. You knew he was going to
be a star in the NHL. He could do whatever he wanted on the ice.
I don't know how many times every game he would grab the puck
behind the net and just streak down the ice and deke everyone.

It's funny to look back on so many of the notable junior
players I played with and against. Larry Robinson was with the
Kitchener Rangers, for example, but he was so tall and awkward
that I never thought he'd make it. Bob Gainey in Peterborough
was a lot like Robinson. You could see he had talent but hadn't
grown into his body quite yet. They both got so much better
when they went to the pros.

Ed Reigle, who'd played for the Bruins in the NHL and had
coached in Europe, was in charge of the Gens that year, but I
can't say if he was a good coach or not, because I was distracted
and didn't concentrate. My mind was mush. Yet I played in parts
of 52 games (15 wins, 28 losses, 4 ties). It was really strange that no
one noticed how distant I was from it all.

The most notable thing, besides my love life, was the arrival of

Mike Amodeo to the Gens in early January, in exchange for Teddy McComb, meaning that I was the main goalie. A Scarborough guy from Toronto's east end, Mike had come up through the Marlies organization. He knew how to speak his mind and had spent time in both Hamilton and Niagara Falls before Toronto sent him to Oshawa. He was a solid defenceman who knew how to take care of business, and we became instant friends.

> **MIKE AMODEO, GENERALS DEFENCEMAN:** We
> hung together, we ate together, all that kind of
> stuff. Everybody has their own personalities, and
> ours meshed.

I was just killing time. In French we say *juste de passer le temps*—just going through life, passing the time. I was there because there was nothing else for me to do. I didn't want to go to school. My girlfriend was part of what kept me in Oshawa, and I was a floater, so Oshawa was the best place for me at that moment. It was what it was.

During the summer, which I spent mainly hanging out at the local swimming pool and playing in a band, I broke up with Marion. As much as that might have hurt, it also meant that I didn't have any distractions. My brother Norm was off to the NHL, and he was determined to get in better shape. Truthfully, it was probably Rick Martin, his best friend and teammate, who came up with the idea. They arranged for three weeks of training at Johnson State College in Vermont and brought me along too. A friend had a mobile home nearby where we crashed.

I was still having a lot of trouble mustering the desire to play hockey. A friend of mine had gone to a hypnotist in Montreal and swore that he'd been cured of car sickness. So I thought, "Fuck, maybe I'll try that." I wanted a hypnotist to convince me that I really had a desire to play hockey, but he could never get me under. I stayed conscious. Instead, he gave me these suggestions. "You love hockey, you want to play." But when I got out of there, I didn't feel any different.

Going back to boring old Oshawa, I was a year older and definitely stronger, and finally the Generals had a coach/general manager that knew how to deal with me. (Ed Reigle had bailed for "personal reasons.") Gus Bodnar had played in the NHL from 1943, when he was named rookie of the year, until 1955, with the Leafs, Blackhawks and Bruins—but he never talked with us about his NHL days. He knew kids, since he'd coached at the Junior C and Junior B levels and graduated to the Junior A Marlboros, taking them to the 1967 Memorial Cup. He also knew how to relate to people—he had a second job as a salesman at a steel company.

Gus got me straightened out. He was a good guy, a father figure. When he talked to you, it was always in a positive way. He never put you down. A real good coach—the guys really liked him. One night in Hamilton, he benched me because I was not concentrating. We won 5–0, and Dennis Higgins, my backup, got a shutout. That woke me up a bit, and when I got back in, I played much better.

> **MIKE AMODEO:** Gus knew how to work his players, how to combine his players, so much. He knew how to get the best out of everybody.

It was a really young club, and I think we had eight rookie forwards and a pair of first-year defencemen. One of those rookies was Bill Lochead, out of Sarnia, Ontario, who'd been the second overall draft pick. Though he got mononucleosis and broke his knuckles punching someone's helmet, limiting him to 37 games, he still netted 27 goals, playing left wing to Bob Ferguson at centre and Rick Middleton on the right side.

Compared to my other two seasons in Oshawa, I was more serious in my third year. I lived with the McCombs, the parents of Teddy McComb. He'd left to go to university at Mount Allison, and they asked me if I wanted to move in—I had other options, but I thought living with an older, quiet family would help me. Well, it helped me learn about people and how hypocritical they can be.

I got to move into Teddy's room and sleep in his bed. Mr. McComb was an institution in Oshawa, a powerbroker in amateur sports, particularly baseball and hockey. I would later learn that he's in the Oshawa Sports Hall of Fame and there's a baseball field named after him in town; when I was there, I was oblivious.

TED McCOMB: My parents didn't take in billets. They took in somebody basically because they were doing him favour, giving him a home the same way they gave me a home.

When they asked me to go their place, I said okay even though I didn't really know them. They pretended to like me, but they didn't. I'll tell you the reason—because I ran their kid out of town. McComb was traded to Toronto during my second year because management believed in French-Canadian goalies, which were the rage at the time. It's the old adage, keep your friends close and enemies closer, and how people can be nice to your face but are actually planning your demise behind closed doors.

What I came to realize when I was living with the McCombs was that the reason they invited me is because they wanted me to fail. They wanted to see my failure. You cannot fool me. They had a nice smile in front of me, but I knew their feelings toward me. I could see it when I had a good game. They had a big smile, but they were fucking burning inside. I could feel it. I'm not fucking stupid. When I had a bad game, they may have said, "Oh, poor Gilles," but they were happy. From that day on, I thought, never again will I be with people like that. The lyrics to John Lennon's "Crippled Inside" come to mind: "One thing you can't hide is when you're crippled inside."

> **TED McCOMB:** When I look back on my experience with him and what I thought was friendship, I'm not impressed, and I really don't have a lot of good things to say. Yes, we were teammates and even to the point where he lived with my parents while I was at university. My parents liked him—he's a likable guy. But at the same time, it was using; he's a user and a manipulator. That's in my rear-view mirror when I look back. I haven't heard from Gilles since he left my parents' place.

In *my* rear-view mirror is a letter Teddy sent me when I was with the Toros, accusing me of forgetting my roots and old friends. I didn't realize we were friends. When we were playing together, I could always sense him wanting me to fail. When he was in net, I rooted for him to succeed since that meant I didn't have to go in, and I thought at that point that I would be going back to Montreal to stay at Christmas.

That third year in Oshawa marked the only time I ever got a tip from a goaltender—Jacques Plante. The Maple Leafs would come once a year to Oshawa to practice. We practiced before them on December 31, the rink packed with fans who'd paid $3 just to watch the Leafs skate. Plante was watching me. I used to play with my stick in a way that left a hole between my legs. Plante kept his stick at his left foot. It's a different stance, and your body weight goes to the left side, leaning forward a bit more, with the stick flatter and covering the five hole. It's subtle, but it worked. It kept me more on my toes, more alert and more aggressive. Just from changing my stance, I got a lot better, just that one tip. When there was a shot, I could move in a way that dragged my pad, so that the puck would hit the pad.

At the time, the philosophy was, of course, that stand-up goaltending was the best style. If you were always down on the ice, you weren't going to get drafted. I tried to be like Johnny Bower, standing up. If the puck was near him, Bower wouldn't fall on it, he'd take a knee and cover it.

It was a quiet, uneventful year. I was well-behaved: I just played and pretended that life was important. The team battled back and forth with the Marlies for first place, but they ran away from us as the season wound down. We finished with a 35–18–10 record, for second.

MIKE AMODEO: We were on a roll that year, and we battled with the big boys. I'm not saying we had an elite team, but we did fairly well for the

team we had . . . Everybody filled a role. Ricky
Middleton, he was pretty slick. Billy Lochead
back in the day. Jumpin' Jack Lynch. Bobby Kirk.
I mean, Bobby Kirk never, ever gets a mention
in anything and he was just a good, solid hockey
player. He was a defenceman. Tough guy, played
the game, played it honest, and wouldn't back
down. He was intricate part of that team.

People weren't as statistic-oriented as they are now. If we were
winning 5-0 with a couple of minutes to go, I would be looking at
the girls in the stands. If they scored a goal, I didn't care. Today,
the goalie wants that shutout so his stats look better. I appeared in
55 games, got 30 wins and one shutout, losing 13, with eight ties,
and a 3.66 goals-against average after surrendering 182 goals. At
the end of the season, the 10 OHA coaches voted on the season's
all-stars, and I was named second-team goalie; Ottawa's Michel
"Bunny" Larocque was the first-team keeper, and I'd be compared
to him throughout my career.

PIERRE GAGNE, LONGTIME FRIEND: They were
so different. Bunny was so serious about his job as
a goalie, he always wanted to improve. Gilles was
much more casual. But Gilles was a better athlete
than Bunny Larocque. Both had good careers.

In the first round of the playoffs, we beat the Niagara Falls Flyers
in a rough best-of-seven series; game five had 200 minutes in
penalties, and the deciding game was only a little less violent,
with 118 minutes and Lochead tossed for pushing a linesman. In

the next round, things started out all right, as we beat Ottawa in the first game even though we were short a couple of suspended players, like Lochead, and both Tom Simpson and Mike Amodeo were out with injuries. Then I got the flu and missed games two and three, both losses. Game four, with me back in the net and feeling like crap, ended in a 2–2 tie. But that was it. Even though thieves had broken into the 67s' dressing room, stolen Larocque's pads and mask, and wrecked a bunch of skate blades—and stolen the hair dryer—they came into Oshawa and doubled us, 4–2. I can still picture the last goal: Tony Herlick shot it from the right point and it deflected way up into the air, and before I could find it, it had fallen into the net. We should have surrendered there, because no one showed up for the 7–0 loss to end our season in the sixth game.

That summer, I had a brief fling as a goaltending teacher at a hockey school, and one of my Generals teammates was there.

BILL LOCHEAD, GENERALS LEFT WING: We were counsellors, teaching the little kids. We had a small cottage, which four of us split. Gilles was in that cottage with us. He could play the guitar really well. It's off-season, you're up in Muskoka in the summer, and we had some really fun singing sessions. He liked to play the Beatles. I remember "Birthday." He got us going. Like Stompin' Tom Connors, I started trying to keep the beat—I couldn't play any instruments, so I just tried to keep a beat, so I was stamping on this little cottage floor so hard my foot went right through the floor.

The teaching part I did okay with—it was all the rest of the time that got me in trouble. I got drunk, and some of the kids were drinking with us, underage. So I got kicked out.

My attention returned to Montreal and wondering what I was going to do with my life. There were only 14 NHL teams at the time, with two more coming in, which meant only 32 jobs as a goalie. Little did I know that a new league would offer me a chance to play professional hockey.

CHAPTER 4

NORM

My brother Norm never came outside to play hockey with us. Most of the people in our town were surprised that he made it to the NHL, playing for the Rangers, Flames, Sabres and North Stars. We used to go outside for road hockey games, but my brother never did. He was hanging out in the woods with his buddies, usually with a bow and some arrows. He was a hunter. Norm never watched hockey, never played with us. He was weird.

He's also gone. He drank himself to death in 2010, living alone, reading books or playing Legend of Zelda—no kidding, he must have saved that princess hundreds of times.

I've struggled with what to write about him. If my two older brothers, Jacques and Norm, hadn't gotten into hockey, would I have become a player? I can't say that either were especially encouraging of my own hockey skills. Norm was naturally talented in a way that I never was. He was strong and solid, and bigger than me.

One of his friends was Dan Bouchard, who would play in the NHL too. They were in the same class and played on the same hockey and baseball teams in LaSalle. They both excelled in school.

> **DAN BOUCHARD:** Let's say the teacher put some problems on the board. Well, we would rush to do it so we could go back to reading Bob Morane. Bob Morane was an adventure guy, and Norm would just read, read, read. He could read a mile a minute. I used to read sports stories, about famous athletes around the world. We used to go to the library and put that inside our school books and read. Norm's problem was he was bored with school because he knew so much, he was so intelligent.

On the ice, he was a great skater who could pass with accuracy and kill penalties. He was never the star of the team, but he could be counted on for some goals with his left-handed shot. After playing minor hockey in the church league in LaSalle, and Junior B with Thetford Mines Junior Canadiens, he moved up to the Montreal Junior Canadiens in 1968. At one time, it was stacked with prospects for *Les Canadiens* but that changed with the NHL expansion in 1967, and the arrival of the entry draft. The Junior Canadiens, playing as a part of the Ontario Hockey Association, won the Memorial Cup both years he was there, in 1969 over the

Regina Pats and then against the Weyburn Red Wings. That 1969 team is often called the greatest junior team of all time, with the likes of Gilbert Perreault, Richard Martin, Marc Tardif, Réjean Houle, Ian Turnbull, Jocelyn Guevremont and tough guy André Dupont. Many had played together in Thetford Mines.

Norm was a first-round pick by the New York Rangers, 11th overall. He got a $10,000 signing bonus. The Rangers assigned him to the Omaha Knights of the Central Hockey League, where the coach was Fred Shero, who would later lead the Philadelphia Flyers to a couple of Stanley Cups. Again, he arrived on a team loaded with talent, including Pierre Jarry, Bill Hogaboam, Michel Parizeau, Ab DeMarco and André Dupont. The Knights won the league that year. The following season, he got into three games for the Rangers, but spent the rest of the time in Omaha.

While in Nebraska, Norm met Robin McGilpin. Her father, Colonel William A. McGilpin, Jr., was in the Air Force and was a big hockey fan. He introduced Norm to his daughter. The young couple moved together to Atlanta when Norm was claimed in the 1972 expansion draft, the fourth pick by the Flames, after goalies Phil Myre and his buddy Dan Bouchard, and defenceman Kerry Ketter. Norm and Robin married in December of that year. I was at my grandfather's house when we got the call from Norm to tell us the news. My mom had only met Robin once and was furious that he had gotten married without telling her ahead of time, especially to an 18-year-old English-speaking American. My dad didn't give a shit. They had a daughter, Chantal, two years later, born in Buffalo. I was named her godfather. She was a very sick baby, and her trachea and esophagus were fused together in some places. Chantal was a fighter, though, and survived.

CHANTAL PUYLEART: I do remember going to the games. I was very small. I remember sometimes Norm would take me out onto the ice and skate me around a little bit . . . he would have moments of playfulness, I would say. I can remember watching *Looney Tunes* with him, or him just sitting on the floor playing with me. But then there were times when he and my mom were, to put it nicely, not getting along. He just wasn't caring for his family.

Norm fit in fine with his various teams, especially as his English improved. Like me, he enjoyed a laugh, which endeared him to teammates.

The flip side was that his love of reading was downright confounding to the other players. If my brother was reading a book and you asked him a question about it, you'd have to shake him to get his attention. In French, we say *dans la lune*. That means he was absent-minded. Guys were telling me in Buffalo that when it was his time to jump onto the ice, sometimes he'd just sit there and the coach would have to shake him because his mind was elsewhere.

DAN BOUCHARD: His first marriage failed because I think he read too much. He'd be home and sit there with a book and ignore everything around him. He would read novels, two or three a week. For a hockey player in those days—shoot, some of them never read a whole book in their whole life. It was very, very unusual.

In Atlanta, the coach, Bernie "Boom-Boom" Geoffrion, just gave up on Norm, and he was keeping the end of the bench warm when Buffalo's Punch Imlach traded for him on Valentine's Day 1973. Norm hadn't played a game since December 20, and his confidence was buoyed when the Sabres put him in the lineup regularly. After a couple of decent seasons in Buffalo, he was dealt to the Minnesota North Stars, where his NHL career petered out. His stats were respectable: 39 goals, 44 assists in 201 games; a single assist in six playoff games.

Norm and his first wife, Robin McGilpin. *Courtesy Chantal Puyleart*

Norm and Robin settled in Buffalo after his career ended, but it was not an easy life. He didn't want to work and was a lost cause. I probably sent $10,000 to Norm between 1977 and 1978. Then I told him that I wouldn't send him any more money. When they ran out of money and therefore couldn't buy food, Robin and Chantal left, moving to Florida, where Robin's parents lived.

CHANTAL PUYLEART: When I was little and we left, my quote to everybody when they asked where my dad was, my answer would be that "my daddy likes Buzzweiser." I knew at a young age that that was a problem. But I still wanted a dad, I still wanted my father very much. It was very confusing for me too, because even though my mom is an American and an English-speaker, I was around French a lot. Growing up basically in the southern United States and having to explain my name every week, that was my life.

Not too long afterward, I got a call from Rick Martin, who had played hockey with Norm for years, dating back before junior hockey. Rick and Norm were like soulmates when they were younger, and they would spend their summers training together and playing golf. Rick was concerned about Norm and needed my help. I called Donald, my brother-in-law, to make the trip with me to Buffalo. We left ridiculously early, at four in the morning, with the intention of being home that night.

Rick had told us that Norm had a room on the second floor of a friend's bar, so we went in there, and the owner told us that Norm was upstairs reading in his room. Sure enough, that's where we found him. From there, it was even more bizarre. He wouldn't respond when we talked to him, or even acknowledge we were there. I went down to the bar owner and asked for a few garbage bags. Donald and I went around the depressing room and tossed what few belongings Norm had into the bags, mainly books and clothes. Then we just grabbed him and took him downstairs to the car. He offered no resistance. Believe it or not, on our way back to LaSalle that evening, he read all the way.

Norm stayed at my parents' until he got back on his feet. He went back to school, got a job and got married again, to Mireille, in 1980. Their son, Jonathan, was born in 1981. Eventually, he found a good job as a purchasing agent for a company that built jails, based in New York State. That was the last place he worked. His marriage to Mireille fell apart because he would go hunting for a week or two without telling her. One time, I was visiting my brother Jacques at his boyfriend's house in Saint-Polycarpe, and in walked Norm, all done up for hunting, with the camouflage gear and face paint. He'd slept in the woods all night. He came in, said hello, got some water and food and left again.

My parents, François and I stayed in touch with Robin and Chantal, certainly far more than Norm did. Robin remarried, and Chantal changed her last name to her stepfather's, Harmon. Norm didn't contest the adoption at all.

CHANTAL PUYLEART: He never emotionally or financially supported me after I left with my mom. Even if he did start working, he never made any moves to make amends.

Looking back, I'm pretty sure his battle with the bottle started in Thetford Mines. You're just a teenager, away from home, and in a rough mining town like that, booze is plentiful and almost a necessity. There were alcoholics on my mom's side of the family, so it wasn't something we were unfamiliar with. Jacques, Claudine, François and I all missed that gene; it was like Norm was doing all the drinking for the five of us.

In the last five years of his life, I used to buy his cigarettes at the native reserve near where I live. He could hardly walk because his arteries were hardening from all the drinking, and his circulation was the shits. I wanted to take him to the hospital, but he wasn't interested in living anymore. I think that's something that's plagued our family—a lack of interest in life.

> **FRANÇOIS GRATTON:** I took care of Norm a lot when he quit his job. I would give him money each week so he could eat. I have to thank his landlord, Francine, since she didn't kick him out. He was paying only his rent (not his utility charges), that's all he could do, with the little bit of money he had. The last two years that he was alive, I would stop by his place: "Let's go to Loblaws and buy some food." He would have ended up in a park, a beggar on the street.

When he went down, he went down fast. I remember Claudine calling and telling me that Norm had to go to the hospital or he'd be dead before Christmas. I visited him, tried to get him to go get checked out, but he didn't want to go. After that, I phoned my other brothers and told them that Norm was on his way out and there was nothing we could do about it. He died December 10, 2010. His son had to look after all the arrangements, which is strange, because Norm really had nothing to do with raising either of his kids. There wasn't a funeral right away, just a mass in April 2011 so Chantal could make it up from Atlanta. She had recently given birth and didn't want to travel up with her newborn son, Ryan, right away.

> **CHANTAL PUYLEART:** Norm never asked about his grandson, never asked about my son. François

In happier times, here's my wife, Anne; Norm's oldest daughter, Chantal; Norm holding my son William; and Norm's son Jonathan.
Courtesy Claude Bertrand

shared with my dad that Ryan looked a little bit like him.

I'm not sure anyone from the NHL noticed or cared. Some old friends from around Montreal came out for the mass. His best buddy, Rick Martin, died three months after Norm, his heart giving out while he was driving in Buffalo in March 2011.

There's little doubt in my mind that he had a few concussions through the years. After all, he played in an era without helmets, and they tested Martin's brain and found chronic traumatic encephalopathy, the bangs to the brain that cause weird behaviour and memory issues. Norm was nowhere near the star that Rick was and spent many more years in the tougher minor leagues. At the end, Norm was depressed and didn't want to live. Besides the alcoholism, who knew what other demons existed in his mind—he wasn't one to share.

CHAPTER 5

GOING NATIONAL

If someone tells you that they really believed the World Hockey Association would work, they are full of shit. No one did. I was there, in 1972—one of the players who made the decision to try the upstart league, out-of-nowhere competitors to the established NHL. Personally, I didn't think that the WHA would survive. I figured that by January, I'd be on the beach in Florida—that the league would fold.

To get the jump on the NHL, the WHA held its draft on February 13, 1972. I was selected by the Edmonton Oilers, and my brother Norm, who was New York Rangers property but playing in the minors in Omaha, was taken by Dayton. That team never played a game there and soon relocated to Houston. Since I was still playing with the Generals, I didn't give the next step a lot of thought; I don't think anybody really thought about WHA draft picks at that point. It was a bunch of pretend hockey owners putting together lists of players.

The NHL Entry Draft was a couple of months later, in June, and the Buffalo Sabres selected me in the fifth round. Punch Imlach, who was running the Sabres, offered me $5,000 to sign, $8,000 to play my first year and $10,000 the second year, and a ticket to the Central Hockey League. I told him, "I will make more money playing with my band." It wasn't quite true, but it was close.

"That's it," I decided; "I'm not playing hockey." But then the WHA started to get some momentum, and it actually seemed like it might really happen. In September, the Oilers (who had offered me $54,000 over two years) traded my rights to the Ottawa franchise. The general manager of the Nationals, Buck Houle, called me and offered ridiculous numbers for a rookie goalie who hadn't even been the best in the OHA: $20,000 to sign, $25,000 the first year and $30,000 the second. Do the math: that was $75,000 for two years. I had no money; I was broke and out of junior hockey. It was a no-brainer.

I asked Buck Houle for No. 69. He said no. Then I asked for No. 33, and he said he'd think about it, because in those days the numbers were always 1 to 30. It was a total revolution to go to No. 33.

Houle and the Nationals announced the signing of three goalies—me, veteran Les Binkley, who was 36 and expected to be the starter, and rookie Frank Blum out of Junior B—on the same day that Billy Harris was signed to coach. Harris—Hinky was his nickname, but I called him Billy—had played in the NHL and had recently been coaching in Europe. (Don't confuse him with the Billy Harris who is my age and who I played junior hockey against.) With the 1972 Summit Series going on, international

GILLES GRATTON

WORLD HOCKEY ASSOCIATION

Here I am, a rookie in the WHA. *International Hockey Archives*

hockey was hot, and Harris was seen as a good hire. He certainly was for me.

The only NHLers on the Nats were Wayne "Swoop" Carleton, Binkley and Guy Trottier. The rest of the lineup was filled with a few journeymen minor-leaguers and a ton of raw players right out of junior. Only a few of us spoke French, though: me, Trottier, Bob Charlebois and Bobby Leduc.

BOB CHARLEBOIS, LEFT WING: We were all getting to know one another, I think you have to remember that. The first year in Ottawa, we were bodies coming in from everywhere.

Houle really believed in youth and a team growing together. My Oshawa buddy, Mike Amodeo, was signed too, so I had a room-mate and running mate; Tom Simpson came from the Gens too. Other guys I'd faced in the OHA, so I knew them a little, like Gavin Kirk of the Marlies and Pat Hickey of the Red Wings.

> **RICK SENTES, LEFT WING:** I was 26 and they were all 20, 21. All in all, there were some real good rookies in Hickey, Amodeo, Rick Cunningham on defence, Gilles in net. He was a different kind of person. That was my sixth year pro. I'd never met anyone as different as he was. But in net, he could stand on his ear for 10 games in a row and then have one bad game.

> **GAVIN KIRK, CENTRE:** We were a fairly young group. We just had a great time and enjoyed our lives. I think there were six or eight rookies on the team. These are all guys that don't have a wife and family yet . . . you can't believe that you're getting paid more than what a lot of the NHL players were making then.

Since I was expecting to be the backup goalie, I didn't think I'd play much. To that end, I made only a half-hearted attempt to get into game shape. But life really played a trick on me. Right after the first game of the year—actually the first ever WHA regular season game, at Ottawa's Civic Centre against the Oilers— Binkley got hurt (a common theme) and the responsibility fell on my shoulders, which I didn't expect at all.

Fuck, I'm up.

I wasn't exactly filled with confidence. Gavin Kirk tried to encourage me. I replied that I didn't think we'd ever win another game. In the end, I had 25 wins, 22 losses and three ties that season.

Bink really was my saviour, but I know I drove him nuts.

> **MIKE AMODEO:** Les and Gilles worked exceptionally well. They were really good friends. And there was no animosity who was starting. They both wanted to play all the time, but they were really good buddies.

Les was a calming influence and never seemed to be nervous. He was a little like Gordie Howe, one of those guys who has a dry sense of humour. He was always making jokes but not laughing, keeping a straight face.

> **LES BINKLEY, GOALIE:** Gilles was eccentric. We'd be sitting beside each other tightening our skates. He'd say, "Jesus, Mars is going to collide with Jupiter tonight. I don't know if I'm going to be okay or not." Here I am tightening my skates a little bit tighter because I figure I'm going to get in the game sometime.

The stories get exaggerated and repeated through the years, but it's true that I used to read my horoscope and the astrological signs, and that would affect my mood and my thinking. And if a goalie is not focused, not in the right mood to perform, then why would you put him in net? The astrology could be used for good, though.

TOM MARTIN, RIGHT WING: He could read
the signs. "I can tell anybody's sign within 10
minutes." He would go into all the things about
what the signs meant. None of us were into that.
One day we took him to a bar. We went around
and got seven or eight girls no one knew. We told
them, "This is not a pickup thing or anything, we
just don't believe he can do this." They all said
okay. He talked to each one for five minutes, and
then he picked the signs for each one—he got
every one right.

At the time, I had two bullshit things to get girls into my bed.
I used to play the piano, and that worked pretty well, especially if
I crooned a song. Another one was my knowledge of *The Urantia
Book*. I remember talking with a girl in Winnipeg for a couple
of hours in the bar about the book, and she was so blown away
that she jumped in bed with me right away. I'd been reading it
since I was 15 years old. It's a lot to digest, since it's about super-
universes, mixing science with religion and philosophy, but it was
right up my alley.

The media also started to realize that I didn't speak hockey
talk. There was no "give 110 per cent" bullshit from me.

GAVIN KIRK: We had a press conference, and
Gilley and I went. He was doing really well as a
rookie, and I was as well, so the two of us attended
this meet-the-players type luncheon. They asked
us a couple of questions. One of the questions
they asked Gilley was, "You're going to be playing

Bobby Hull next week. His nickname is the
famous Golden Jet. Do you have a nickname?"
Gilley looked and thought for a second, "Well,
they call me the Golden Hammer."

You can only laugh at some of the memories from the WHA.
Over the three years I was there, teams came and went like leaves
blowing in the wind. In Cleveland, the arena still had the chicken
wire instead of panes of glass, like a throwback to another era.
You'd try to avoid skating around too close to the stands during
warm-up because people would spit on us. I had long hair and a
ponytail, so I stood out. "Gratton, you fag," was just one of the
things I'd hear. The other thing with the chicken wire was that
it was unpredictable. The puck would hit it, and you didn't know
where it would go. That's really tough on a goalie.

When we played a team in San Diego, we were able to hop
across the border to Tijuana. About seven or eight of us were
drinking in a bar and thought we had made arrangements to get
blow jobs in the back room. As a group, we go to the back, pay
the girls and—nothing. The girls refuse. One of our veterans got
really pissed about getting ripped off, and just as he's venting,
four or five guys with knives come out of the woodwork. "Okay
guys, no problem. Keep the money. We're leaving." That was a
scary night, tense, and we sobered up quickly.

I was witness to some pretty monumental fights too. Wayne
Carleton, who could really pound them back, once destroyed
Steve Warr in a bar for being a little too loose with his lips about
tales from the road. Tables were flying, and it took four or five of
us to calm Wayne down. Another time, after a game in L.A., we
were in Buck Houle's suite. I was playing the piano and guys were

singing. Boom! A table goes flying. Carleton was standing over Buck Houle. He was just towering over him—he was 6-foot-3. "You trade me tomorrow morning!" Cooler heads prevailed, thankfully, since Carleton was far and away our best player, and finished 23 points ahead of our next-best scorer, Gavin Kirk, at the end of the season.

On the ice, there were angry moments too. We were playing Winnipeg in January 1973, and the Jets were led by Bobby Hull. Our fan base had started to build at the Civic Centre, and they were certainly passionate. We ended up losing 5–4, and referee Pierre Belanger had to be escorted out of the building by eight security guards. He'd been accosted by fans—one reached over the glass and ripped at his hair after a disallowed goal—and by me; I'd chased him down to the timekeeper's bench after I stopped a shot by Norm Beaudin but Belanger called it a goal.

That wasn't even the worst referee moment. One time in Chicago, Brent Casselman was the referee. A player took a shot, and I went down on my knees with my glove in front of me, and I grabbed the puck. I was probably two metres out of my net, way out. Casselman called it a goal, but I had the puck in my glove—and I even showed him. I guess he saw a piece of tape in the net or something. It was the strangest event in my on-ice hockey career, ever. Unbelievable. Fucking guy was out to lunch. I still wonder how he managed to screw that one up.

The travel was a nightmare in the early days of the WHA. One time it took us 10 hours to get from Ottawa to New York. A vehicle on the ground had driven into the plane during a snowstorm. That was the longest trip ever. We got to Madison Square Garden late, but the game still went on (we lost 7–5). There weren't too many people there, maybe 2,000.

Two weeks later, on New Year's Eve, we left Chicago for a game in Quebec City, and it was even more of a marathon. Our connecting plane in Montreal was snowed in, so we had to take a train, with nothing but candy bars and potato chips as nourishment. After that 12-hour trek, big surprise, we lost 8–4.

We often had tons of time to kill on those road trips and entertained ourselves as best we could. There were different factions. Swoop and Bink were buddies, and also close in age, for example. There were the young guys, like me, off raising hell. There were family men like Guy Trottier, and cerebral mysteries like Brian Conacher, who never seemed a part of the team.

TOM MARTIN: You might play a game, which is a five-hour chunk. If you're on the road for two weeks, the rest of the time you're travelling, you're sitting in a hotel. Some guys would play cards, some guys would go out and do touring. A way of relaxing was pulling pranks on each other. All the things that we would do . . . There was one time at the Los Angeles airport. There was a walkway up above, and they were up there fooling around. Mike, Gilles and I said, "Wait a minute!" So we got skate laces and we tied them on my hands and tied them on my feet, and we put the skate laces up the other storey. They got up and made me their puppet. People would come by and they would pull my hand. Of course, after about 15 minutes, people were going by laughing, and then the security came. I said, "Look, I've got nothing to do with it. I know these guys, and they just

> put these laces on me." They took them and Billy
> Harris had to go into the office at the airport
> and say, "Hey guys, it was just a prank. We're just
> having fun."

Me and Amodeo were inseparable and were responsible for so much shit it's almost unbelievable. Some of it was real shit too. We organized a contest over who could have the biggest turd. We'd call other players in to show them and let them be the judges.

We spent five days in Houston, and me and Amodeo, we destroyed the room. It started off innocently enough, two chairs at a table so we could arm wrestle. Then a table leg broke, and it spiralled from there. Guys were coming in and fighting, and we broke both beds, furniture and the television. We were summoned to Buck Houle's room, and he showed us the letter addressed to "Mr. Stratton and Anodea"—it wasn't Gratton and Amodeo. The bill was $10,000. Buck says, "We're going to pay. It's the last time." Hardly.

> **MIKE AMODEO:** The part I know about is as long
> as you showed to play and you were in good shape
> to play, everything was good.

The New England Whalers played in the Boston Garden the first year, before moving to Hartford. We were coming out of the Garden after practice, and there was a line of cabs in front of the building. We see a cabbie sleeping in the car, and his window is down about 10 inches. Amodeo and I creep up really close to the window and scream as loud as we could. The cabbie jumped and hit his head on the top of the car. We were laughing and

Some things have never changed in hockey, like trying to get in front of the goalie! Here Ken Stephanson (#4) and Brian Gibbons (#6) bring down Brian Smith of the Houston Aeros, with Gord Labossiere lurking to my right. *International Hockey Archives*

laughing, but then the guy gets out of his car, goes to his trunk and grabs a crowbar. Fuck, did we ever run, we were scared for our lives. He never caught us, though. He wasn't in good shape.

There was just so much time on the road. Once, we were gone for 29 days. Five days in San Diego. Five days in L.A. Five days in Vancouver. Five days in Edmonton. Five days in Winnipeg. There would be practice on the off day, but not on the travel days. We would do anything, like stunts from *Jackass*. Amodeo and I would go to bars, and we'd piss on the floor while we were drinking. It was like a dare.

A story that has developed a life of its own over the years developed when, unbeknownst to be, Mike paid a Cleveland cab driver with Canadian Tire money.

> **TOM MARTIN:** I was in the lobby and we were all standing around. All of a sudden, they come running in. You say hi to them, and they just ran right in and jumped in the elevator. Everyone just kind of said, "That's weird." Then this cabbie comes in holding this money. "Where did those guys go?" We could see it was all Canadian Tire money. Sort of a typical Amodeo/Gilles story.

The worst part was it was 1973, and we were wearing platform shoes. It was really difficult, but boy did we run.

When I was home, it was a different world. I lived with my Aunt Julienne and Uncle Jean-Paul in the Sandy Hill part of Ottawa, east of downtown. My cousins Pierre and Carmen were a little younger than me but still proved to be good company. My aunt was a very good cook. That year, I think I went from 155 pounds to 172 pounds, so I gained a lot of weight and filled out into the body of a 20-year-old. From their house, I used to walk a few blocks to the Rideau Canal, and I would skate to practice in my goalie skates, and then skate back.

The Nats started to rally after a tantrum by Harris in February got him a $500 fine by the league. After a 2–1 loss to the Philadelphia Blazers on a goal that shouldn't have counted, he said that the WHA didn't want Ottawa in the playoffs. Everyone liked Harris, even if we didn't understand him all the time. (Or hear him—he spoke softly and even blew his whistle lightly at practice.) He was a bit elitist, an intellectual, and we were hockey players.

> **MIKE BOLAND, RIGHT WING:** Billy was
> standoffish. I don't think Billy had a relationship
> with any player, not that I know of. Billy Harris
> was bordering on pseudo-erudite. He had control,
> and Billy knew everything. He never would raise
> his voice. He'd give everybody a long rope. He
> was not a screamer or a yeller, perhaps to his
> detriment. He was probably too nice a guy. But
> he was distant.

Billy was a good coach, sure, but he also served as a father figure to me. It took a while for the guys to buy into his system, but once they did, we were tough to beat. It was a system that was sort of a defensive trap—before anyone ever called it that. We waited for the breaks, with a tight defense, rather than being aggressive. He taught them how to be responsible defensively, but didn't happen overnight. In particular, Brian Gibbons, Steve Warr, Rick Cunningham and Amodeo grew by leaps and bounds on the blue line.

Assisting Billy was Gilles Leger, who we called "Rent-A-Coach." Since Billy kept a home in Toronto, it was often left to Gilles to run practices. When he wasn't helping on the ice, he was helping in the ticket office doing group sales for the team. It's highly doubtful you'd find an assistant coach doing that now in the NHL!

We went 15–7 over our final 22 games. Bink won the first few before getting injured, and I closed out the year as we fought to get into the East Division playoffs. One of the papers dubbed me "Saint Gilles," but it never stuck.

The behind-the-scenes issues were getting as many headlines as we were. Nationals owners Doug Michel and Nick Trbovich had been making noises about moving the team to Toronto or Milwaukee just about all season, since the fans didn't start turning out until we started winning—imagine that. We were told that they needed more than 7,000 fans to break even for a game, and for those early games we were only drawing 2,000. But when the team got humming and the people started showing up, the greedy bastards running the Civic Centre—the Central Canada Exhibition Association—asked for $100,000 to use the arena for each playoff game. The solution was ridiculous, in retrospect—play our "home" games five hours from Ottawa at Toronto's Maple Leaf Gardens, an even *bigger* location.

> **BOB CHARLEBOIS:** We were given 48 hours' notice to our families that we'd be moving to Toronto, to be ready, that we'd be staying in a hotel for the playoffs. That's the kind of warning we got. We just ran out of town. It was a sad thing to leave the city in that way.

The New England Whalers beat us up pretty bad, four games to one in the series. They were a much better team, and they'd win the first-ever Avco Cup with stars like Larry Pleau, Tom Webster, Ted Green, Ricky Ley, Jim Dorey and Al Smith in net.

There might have been a thousand fans at those games against the Whalers at the Gardens, so they were another financial failure.

What those games did do, however, was lay the groundwork for the Toronto Toros.

To blow off steam after it was all over, a bunch of the Nats went to the Bahamas. We spent a lot of time in the casino in Nassau, and a lot of time drinking. That blurred my judgment and almost cost me my career. One night, I left the casino loaded and hopped on my rented motorbike. At some point I hit a tree that was lying on the road, and I flew into the air. I came down hard, landing on my hands. I had sore wrists for about two years, though I never told management.

CHAPTER 6

THEY CALL ME THE STREAK

As the season was ending, we learned that the Ottawa Nationals were moving. That didn't sit well with the guys. And it was one of the reasons we lost in the playoffs. We were distracted. Who are you playing for? You just played in front of 10,000 people for a few weeks, and suddenly you go to Toronto and there are just 1,500—no one was interested; win or lose, what's the difference? There was an outpouring of emotion from the fans of Ottawa thrilled by the rise of their team, and even a cynic like me wasn't immune to it.

Officially, owners Nick Trbovich and Doug Michel put the team up for sale at the 1973 WHA meetings, and it was John F. Bassett who stepped forward to lead a group of investors to raise the $1.8 million needed to buy the Nats and move them to

Toronto. Bassett was a big name in Toronto. His family owned the *Toronto Telegram* newspaper, for one thing, but his interests stretched into other media, including producing films, and even into tennis, where he was still a competitive player. There were 26 initial investors in the about-to-be-named Toronto team. Bassett believed that a WHA franchise in town could compete with the established Toronto Maple Leafs. Fans were asked for team name suggestions, and the Toros were born in June 1973.

The bulk of the team was the same, Billy Harris coaching, with Wayne Carleton as the leader, and Tom Martin, Guy Trottier, Gavin Kirk, Tom Simpson, Jack Gibson, Bob Leduc and the like on forward, and Mike Amodeo, Rick Cunningham and Steve Warr back on the blue line. Newcomers included Wayne Dillon, an 18-year-old centreman straight off the Toronto Marlies, who would play a key role in my life, Pat Hickey of the Hamilton Red Wings, Peter Marrin of the Marlies and Steve Cuddie, who the Toros got from the Winnipeg Jets.

The owners thought that a few players with historical ties to the Leafs would help, so Carl Brewer was brought in on defense, and former NHL Rookie of the Year Brit Selby was hired, as a left winger; Bassett even tried to get Darryl Sittler. Brewer especially made a big difference—he was the best defenceman I ever played with; it was unreal how good he still was.

One night in Varsity Arena, Brewer was stationed in front of me. He had holes in his gloves so he could properly grab someone by the shirt without looking like he was doing it. Carl had a hold of one guy, and another came by and Carl stopped *him* with his stick and cleared the puck with his skate. That guy was so good. He saved me so many goals, and he was a calming influence for the entire team.

Me and Amodeo spent a lot of time with Carl, in saunas and stuff, and he told great stories about Punch Imlach being a tyrant. He was so stressed playing for Imlach that he wouldn't have sex during the winter—it was pretty much forbidden. He hated Imlach and basically became a basket case during his time with the Leafs.

As well, Carl was scared of flying, and every time we brought him onto the plane, he was drunk, sedated. One time, we got him on the plane in just his shoes, underwear, tie and socks—that's it. When he wasn't drunk enough, he would sit in the first seat and hold on tight, stressed, breathing heavy. He would drink, drink, drink on the plane. I did my astrological chart, and I told him, "I'm not going to die in a plane crash, so if you're in a plane with me, you're not going to die. Don't be scared, since I'm here."

It was still me and Les Binkley in net on the Toros. For a while after we got to town, we were roommates at a west-end Toronto motel. Despite moving cities, the team didn't help with moving expenses or finding a place to live, at least not from what I remember. But then, I had nothing to move, just one suitcase.

One day, Bassett came to see us at the motel, and he told me, "I don't want you to stay in a motel anymore. You're going to come stay with me." I didn't know Bassett very well at that point. He seemed like a good guy—nice to me, anyway. They had a big house on the Bridle Path—a mansion, really. When I knocked on the door, I was stunned by how beautiful his wife, Susan, was.

I had my own room and bathroom—practically my own wing of the house—so I had my privacy. The benefit was the meals— not eating in restaurants all the time. It was a family life with structure. I was there about half a year.

The Bassetts had long been a media family, owning the *Toronto Telegram* newspaper and founding Baton Broadcasting, which ran Toronto's CFTO station. As the son of privilege, John F. got a chance to work in many different facets of business, including real estate and a software company, and liked being in the spotlight. He and Susan had four children: John C., Carling, Vicky and Heidi.

Stable family life was new to me, and I definitely used it later with my two kids—there was structure, a framework, and they'd know where the line was crossed with behaviour. I never had that with my parents. They let me do whatever I wanted. I was never shown how to behave, and I learned a lot living with the Bassetts. Sure they were rich, but they were not unbearable snobs by any means. In fact, I became very fond of them. Some nights, I would go and kiss the girls goodnight. Of course, years later Carling became a huge tennis star.

Their high-class friends found me to be a fascinating character, so I was definitely moving in a different crowd. On the road, I was still pretty crazy.

One weekend, my buddies Claude and Mike Bertrand came to town to visit. We sat down with Vicky to work on a song called "The Flying Horse" that she had written lyrics for. I helped her put it to music and we recorded it on this tiny recorder. With a grand piano in the living room, I'd often have singing sessions with the Bassetts.

Montreal Canadiens goaltender Ken Dryden was sitting out the 1973–74 season, articling at a law firm in Toronto. He came to dinner at the Bassetts' three or four times while I was staying there.

John told me he wanted to sign Dryden.

I told him, "You might as well trade me, if you're going to sign Dryden."

He says, "No, no, I want the two best goaltenders in the world on my team."

Uh huh, sure. Of course, Dryden went back to Montreal and won more Stanley Cups, and I continued to be a fuck-up. In January 1974, the Cincinnati Stingers, who were entering the league the following season, actually tried to land me. My agent, Dave Schatia, even talked with Imlach and the Buffalo Sabres, who still held my NHL rights. I guess word had travelled throughout hockey that Bassett was after Dryden. To be honest, I found Ken kind of dull and lacking in charisma, but his goal-tending skills were out of this world.

I don't know what went on behind the scenes with the arena situation. We'd played in Maple Leaf Gardens in the playoffs when we were still the Nationals, and then we got downgraded to the University of Toronto's Varsity Arena with the Toros. My first game at Varsity, I was late, because I got lost. When I got in, everybody was dressed and were heading out to the ice for warm-up. While it was not a big, fancy arena by any means, there was great atmosphere at Varsity, with the fans crammed in there—it maybe sat 5,000. It was also probably the coldest arena I ever played in. It was there that I started taking all my equipment off and changing my sweaty underwear between periods. Later, in the big NHL arenas, I didn't do that.

The Nationals weren't the only team to switch locations in the WHA. The New York Raiders gave up on playing at Madison Square Garden and moved in November. They became the Knights, playing in the small town of Cherry Hill, New Jersey, at this rinky-dink arena. We had to change into our uniforms at the hotel. But there were benefits to playing there too. Poochie was the name of a hooker in Cherry Hill, and she was pretty good-looking too. One of the older guys would get a case of beer, set up a chair, and hand out bottles of beer as she gave blow jobs in a room while the team stood in line in the hallway, drinking and waiting their turn. Another guy would have a timer, and it was a competition to see who could last the longest—it certainly wasn't me; she was that good.

Early in the season, Coach Harris told Paul Patton of the *Globe and Mail* that "the team plays better when Gratton is in than they do in front of Binkley." I often wondered about that. Was it because I was young and untested? Or was my style different?

PAT HICKEY, LEFT WING: The one thing with Gilles back there is that you had more time, more concentration on your own game to do what you did best and be creative. Back then with the Toros, we were all creative and innovative and free and encouraged to do what you do best. Come game time, there was no way you were going influence Gilles Gratton. He was either there and you had confidence in him or not. Most of the time, he was there, so we never really had to think. Binkley was more of a coach. Bink actually wanted the wingers to do certain things, and he let you know. If he wanted you coming back deeper into the zone for whatever reason, whether it was with the coach's strategy or design, we basically followed Bink. So there was a percentage of time where we were always trying to cater to Bink . . . He was a guy that you loved, so maybe, in a way, you did

play more defensive and more thinking about,
"What are my responsibilities back there? Because
I don't want Bink to be beat up on."

Binkley and I shared a 3–0 shutout in what was the most violent
game I was ever a part of.

The scene was Los Angeles, our fifth game of the season, and
first win. The Sharks were not a very good team. Bink started
and held down the fort until he was hit by Terry Slater's stick
five minutes into the second period. He stayed in the game for
a bit after that, until I was finally called upon. I made nine saves
the rest of the way, and got a 10-minute misconduct for good
measure.

The win was nice, but what everyone will remember—
including the 3,000 or so in attendance—was the nuttiness during
the last two minutes. Gary Veneruzzo of the Sharks scuffled with
Brewer, and both were sent to the box with 1:41 left in the game.
Veneruzzo then climbed the glass between the penalty boxes to
get at Carl. A fan got into the action and cut Brewer during the
melee as Carl swung his stick around wildly to protect himself.
The ref tossed both Brewer and Veneruzzo, but that didn't settle
anything on the ice.

After play resumed, the brawl started. Ted McCaskill leaped off
the bench and was just running around fucking people up, encouraging his Sharks teammates: "Fight! Fight!" He was a crazy bastard. Amodeo took on three guys. With Bink gone to the dressing
room, both Sharks goalies sat on me and I couldn't move. Steve
Sutherland, the chief Sharks goon, ended up spraying blood from
a gash over his left eye. We had four guys tossed—Brewer, Steve
Cuddie, Amodeo and Brit Selby—and the Sharks lost Veneruzzo,

McCaskill, Sutherland and Earl Heiskala for the remaining minute of the game. The $4,500 in fines levied by the WHA was a league record. Only the goalies didn't get fined.

Bink was just as fragile as he'd been the year before. In November, he ended up with a cast on his right leg, tearing muscles after sprawling to stop Ron Snell of the Winnipeg Jets on a breakaway. Just before that happened, Harris called Bink his number one choice. "Here's what makes Bink terrific," Harris told the *Star*'s Jim Kernaghan early in the season. "He never gets upset and he never sulks. He just plays goal the best he can and if a shot beats him, he plays like it never happened."

I think that was definitely the year when it all came together for me, and I truly became a big-league goaltender. It's true that confidence is a huge part of the game, and even more so for goalies.

MIKE AMODEO: He had just matured. He constantly would work his angles more and more. Originally, he was a reflex goalie, and then as he aged, he had his great reflexes but he worked his positional play much better. I know my first year in junior, mostly it was reflexes. Then in only a year, he was positioning much better in the net at different angles, how to come out. He didn't handle the puck, that's for sure.

As well, I perfected the art of the stall that year.

LES BINKLEY: Gilles had a thing with the trainer all the time. He would call it his "Dead Fish." A guy would go by him and he'd throw himself up

in the air and lay on the ice and roll around. The
trainer would come out, fix him up, and he'd go
back in the net and play again. It's just funny, he
called that his "Dead Fish." We knew about it, but
we didn't know when it was going to happen.

I'd sometimes warn my defensemen, especially Amodeo, with a
little wink, and whisper, *"Poisson mort, poisson mort."* The idea was
that the other team had been in our zone too long, and our guys
were tired. I was being a team player . . .

> **MIKE AMODEO:** Now that is a work of art. Gilles
> would practice his Dead Fish in practice. He sure
> got it down to a science, as so many thought this
> was the real deal. The Dead Fish came out when
> things weren't going so good.

My success in Quebec City continued. I always loved to play in
front of that crowd, with friends and family often making the trip
from Montreal.

> **CLAUDE BERTRAND:** I was a student at the time
> and very, very poor. When Gilles arrived in town,
> he would always invite me to his games. At this
> time, the club slept at the Château Frontenac
> in Quebec City. It was really a nice hotel. Gilles
> would always invite me, and I would sleep there
> in the same room. We always had a great time. It
> was hard for me to see Gilles on the ice playing.
> I found it hard to see the pressure that was on

him when he was the goalie. He would do funny things. The pressure has to go somewhere.

In a 3–1 win on November 22, I stopped 52 shots, including 16 in the first period and 24 in the third, and all the goals came in the third period.

MIKE AMODEO: In my opinion, Gilles Gratton's greatest game that I saw was in Quebec City against the Nordiques. Gilley was always up for a game in his home province. In a pre-game interview with the French press, Gilley said that we were going to win over the Nordiques and they were not going to score. I wish he would have kept that remark to himself.

My buddy stood on his head, just an amazing sight to be seen. As I remember we were totally outshot and outplayed. Everything our backstopper did was perfect. Gilley was in sync mentally and physically, and, of course, the stars were aligned.

Gilley's prediction was on the button—almost. In the last seconds of the third we let our very proud teammate down. Quebec broke the goose egg. We could not clear our end. It seemed like Quebec had more players on the ice than we did. Personally, the only good thing was that I watched the goal from the bench. If I had been on for that goal, I would have had a little explaining to do to my roommate.

After the game, emotions were so high in
the dressing room. The kid was at home, and he
did what he said he would and could: beat the
Nordiques. The press invaded Gilles after the
game, they were in his face. Then it happened all
of a sudden—the stress, pressure, strain, all to be
the best and to live up to your prediction. Gilles
broke down!

Man, I felt for him. We have all had our
moments. As helpless as I was to help my best
friend on the team, I knew what he had just
accomplished was worth it. I asked a few of the
reporters to give Gilley some space and take it
up in a couple of minutes once he had composed
himself. They let up a little but not that much.

Gilles was a little quiet that night, but by the
next morning he was good to go.

Then, at the end of March, back in Quebec City again, the fans
were so furious at the Nordiques that they threw all kinds of shit
onto the ice. I wasn't scared though—I thought it was funny.

PAT HICKEY: The most exciting time in games to
play with Gilles Gratton was when we played in
Le Colisée in Quebec City. He was just dynamite,
because he was passionate and focused. That's
what we used to say about him, "Leave him alone.
Just leave him alone." You could tell in his eyes
that he had this one tonight and he was right in
his fancy place. We'd go out to Winnipeg: "Gilley,

close your eyes. Pretend you're at Le Colisée in Quebec City" to get him into the mood, so we knew that he was actually there.

The Winnipeg Jets, with Bobby Hull front and centre, was tough to play against, but we had their number for the first while, winning the first five games. But man, Hull could shoot, and his shot was like a knuckleball. Once he launched one from the blue line and hit me on the chin; the mask was okay, but he took an inch off where the chin is, and it bruised my neck. The worst shot he had was like he was sweeping the puck, not a slapshot or a wrist shot. He had a big curve and you couldn't see the puck.

Another time he was in the slot, and I came out, and he let that sweep shot go. He hit me in the neck, and the puck stuck there. I went down on the ice. Amodeo put his hand on my neck. If I hadn't turned my head slightly to the right and closed my eyes, I would have been dead. He would have hit me right in the Adam's apple. It went *pap!* You could hear it. I had a circular bruise on my neck for three weeks.

With other teams, it was hard to get pumped up. One time we played against Minnesota in Varsity Arena, and we were leading 10–4 with two minutes to go, and the game ended 10–7. I let in three goals in the last minute because I wasn't paying attention. I didn't care. The guys didn't care. No one was keeping plus/minus stats. The guys only cared if we won.

Then there was a trip to Boston to play the Whalers in January, where my catching glove was stolen. It just disappeared. My other glove was back in Toronto, so I had to borrow one for a couple of games; one game it was Al Smith's, and another, it belonged to the Minnesota Fighting Saints.

THEY CALL ME THE STREAK

Speaking of Smith, when he hurt a hamstring, that meant that I got to play in the WHA All-Star Game on January 3 in Minneapolis. Smith, myself and Gerry Cheevers of the Cleveland Crusaders were the East Division goalies, and we were each supposed to play a period. Instead, Cheevers and I split the job, and we stopped 26 shots as the East beat the West, 8–4. It wasn't really a big deal to me, just another trip, but something different at least.

Not long into 1974, I moved out of the Bassett compound and in with Wayne Dillon and his family. They were in Agincourt, in the northeastern part of Toronto, not far from where the 401 and 404 highways meet. We'd become great friends and he asked me to move in with him and his two brothers. I paid $50 a week.

> **BRIAN DILLON:** Him and Wayne were close. We had the extra bedroom in the house, so that's really how it came about. He was a big part of our family. My parents loved him. It was a big house. My dad had just been promoted to the senior vice-president of Famous Players. He bought his dream home. It was the best two years we had as a family. Even though they do a lot of travelling in hockey, he was always there. All he did was play music.

At the time, Brian was playing centre for my old team, the Oshawa Generals. Somehow Global Television learned about our band and sent a remote truck to the Dillons to do a live segment with us playing. Brian was the lead singer, and I was on rhythm guitar. We did a cover of the Beatles classic "I'll Follow the Sun."

Because of the Generals connection, a radio station in Oshawa started playing it too.

Like in Ottawa, the family atmosphere made for quieter times when the team was at home. And sometimes we liked to spend too much time at the house. Often, Wayne and I would be in our car heading down the Don Valley Parkway for practice and mutually decide that we didn't want to go. These were the days before cell phones, so we'd pull off the highway, find a phone and call in to the team, feigning sickness, then go back north and into bed.

On the road, though, the shenanigans continued.

> **GAVIN KIRK:** Gilley would pull some pranks here and there. He'd get a paper and cut out the different letters and make up different headlines— stuff like that. We used to play a lot of tricks in the airport. We'd take a piece of thread and tape it to a $10 bill and put it out in the middle of the walkway in the airport. He'd be at the other end, and when people saw it and went to grab it, he'd just give it a tug, and they'd almost fall over trying to get it. Anything to keep us busy, because you spent a lot of time in the airports. They were all commercial flights as opposed to charters.

It was during a long trip that year—Vancouver, Edmonton, Winnipeg—that I got crabs. If you have never experienced it, consider yourself lucky. Basically, it's lice in your pubic hair, so it's incredibly itchy and uncomfortable. I got this white stuff to kill the crabs, and I had to shave my pubes. The guys started calling me "the Bald Rat." This is where a real friend comes in handy.

The powder didn't do the complete job, so while we were on the road, Amodeo would get to work. With a hotel lamp positioned for extra light, I'd spread my legs, putting them behind me, so Mike could use tweezers to pick the individual crabs out of my pubic hair. It took a few weeks to clear out and slowed down my wildness on the road.

The whole crabs story speaks to the relationship that Mike and I had, and he did his best to try to understand what made me tick.

> **MIKE AMODEO:** It was in San Diego that Gilles
> introduced me to a new realm of reading. We
> always bought books from the same mystic/occult
> New Age store. I have read and spoken English
> all my life, and I had to read and reread these
> books to make any sense of them. Gilles with
> his "broken English" just breezed through them
> like no tomorrow. I still today have some of these
> books, but I don't think I'll try them again until
> I retire. I'll need lots of time. I will always thank
> Gilles for motivating me to new subject material
> and a better general understanding.

It was funny when teammates looked to me to be responsible. One time, a player begged me to watch out for him: "If I get drunk and you see me start to hustle broads, send me back to my room, please." We found a party on a different floor of the hotel, and sure enough he started to hustle. I tried to get him to leave, and he insisted on staying. Whatever. A few hours later, I wake up with somebody sitting on face. It's a girl sitting on my face! He had brought a girl back to my room.

But there is little doubt that my most famous stunt was skating naked. Streaking was a fad in the 1970s, but there's a lot more to the story than that. First off, it wasn't at Maple Leaf Gardens, as has been passed down through the years, and it wasn't during a game. It was at George Bell Arena, where we practiced, in Toronto's west end. I played a lot of road hockey while at the Dillons' and asked the trainer for a dozen sticks to share with neighbourhood kids. He challenged me: "Streak and you can have the sticks."

I actually asked Tom Martin to come with me, but he didn't want to, as he thought he'd be sent to the minors. So, wearing only my skates and my mask, I headed out into the cold for a couple of freeing laps and a quick pirouette at centre ice. My little sacrifice scored a dozen sticks for my friends and has helped keep my legacy alive.

Just before the playoffs, we were in a bar and someone had a bag of cookies. I'd been drinking beer, so I was hungry and I had two. After the second cookie, my head just went *bang!* and fell down onto the table. I couldn't move. I was paralyzed. There was hash in the cookies. This girl was right beside me, and Pat Hickey is telling her, "This guy is a romantic and is so lonely." With my head on the table, she bends down and says, "I'll make you happy." And I can't move, and just want to tell her to fuck off and leave me alone. But Hickey wouldn't stop, and kept laughing throughout. Finally, they carried me out and brought me back to my place.

And yet we still continued to play hockey, and play surprisingly well. I had one of my best games at the end of the season,

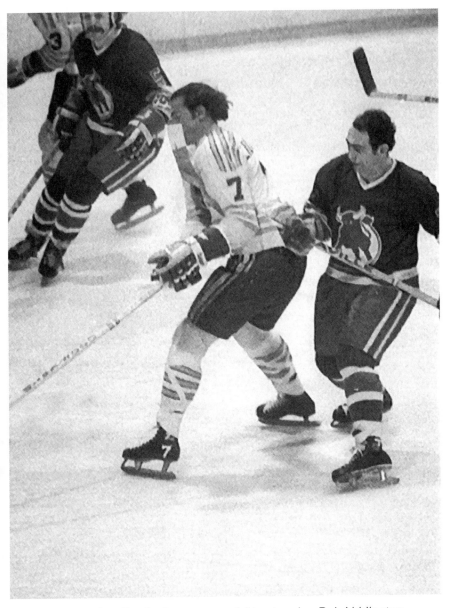

Guy Trottier is unsuccessful in stopping Bob Liddington
of the Chicago Cougars as he puts one past me.
International Hockey Archives

our third-last game, in Quebec City on a Saturday night. Fucking guys were out all Friday night drinking, partying—they didn't give a shit. That night, I got 51 shots, and we only had 16, but we beat Quebec 3–1, and they only scored on me with 20 seconds left to go in the game.

The Toros finished second in the East Division, with a record of with 41 wins, 33 losses and four ties, and my record in 57 games was 26 wins, 24 losses and three ties, and a 3.53 goals-against average, with two shutouts. We were lined up against Cleveland in the first round of the playoffs. We'd lost five of eight games to them in the season but were not too worried, even though they had Cheevers in net.

In the first game at Maple Leaf Gardens, we handled them with relative ease, winning 4–0. I also got into a fight, which was rare for me. Skip Krake had pissed me off, and I let loose. Amodeo came into the fray, and Krake ended up on the ice, going into convulsions. It was a scary moment, but he ended up okay. We took the series in five games, and they only put nine pucks past me.

The fourth-place Chicago Cougars, with center Ralph Backstrom as their star, surprised the first-place New England Whalers in the other East semifinal, winning in seven games. We hadn't done well against Chicago in the regular season, losing five of eight, and tying one. In the first game, I just didn't have it, and Bink replaced me partway through, and we won 6–4. That continued for the rest of the series, actually, where I might start and then Bink comes in, or the other way around.

The playoff games in Chicago were at a shopping mall in a Chicago suburb, Mount Prospect, because a *Peter Pan* production

My hair was at its best during my years in Toronto.
International Hockey Archives

had moved into the International Amphitheatre. The rink in Mount Prospect was actually bigger than regulation.

In the end, the Cougars beat us in seven games. In the finale, I stopped 23, but somehow let in four goals in the second period, in a 5–2 loss.

It was disappointing to lose our chance at the final. The Houston Aeros, with Gordie Howe and his sons Marty and Mark, had won the West and would beat Chicago to win the Avco Cup. Imagine the hype that there would have been having Gordie come back to Maple Leaf Gardens, where his kids had also been stars for the Marlies.

CHAPTER 7

THE LOONY TAKES THE STAGE

Our run to the semifinals put the Toros on the sporting map in Toronto, and John Bassett was determined to make even more of an impact. That summer, he went out and signed the legendary Frank Mahovlich and the 1972 Summit Series hero Paul Henderson to contracts. The team was also on the forefront of the impending European influx of talent to the NHL and WHA, bringing in Richard Farda and Vaclav Nedomansky, who had both defected from Czechoslovakia.

He also re-signed me, but only after I'd considered serious overtures from the Buffalo Sabres.

Bassett's initial offer to me was $60,000 a year for five years, plus a $50,000 signing bonus. He wanted us to do the contract without involving my Montreal-based agents, David Schatia and

Larry Sazant. I considered it briefly but ultimately used their services. That turned out great for me, but not for Bassett.

Schatia and Sazant had been in touch with Punch Imlach in Buffalo. His offer was better—$125,000 as a signing bonus, and then $75,000 the first year, $80,000 the second and $85,000 the third. There was a clause in Gilbert Perreault's contract that he had to be the highest-paid Sabre, which was fine with me. I could never stop him in junior hockey either.

Naturally, we went back to Bassett to sweeten his offer. On May 22, it was announced that I had signed a new five-year deal. I got $100,000 to sign and $101,000 salary each year. I don't know how or why the extra thousand was added. What I had specifically asked for and got was a car, and boy was it sweet.

The team rented me a canary-yellow Porsche 911S Targa, with a sales value of $16,670, for the season. Honestly, I got it for its speed, not the status of owning a Porsche. Other players got cars too—Mahovlich had a sporty Mercedes, Rick Cunningham had a Corvette.

Staying a Toro was about more than money and the car, even if that sounds like bullshit. In Toronto, I had my friends and teammates. I was comfortable there and continued to live with the Dillon family, boxing or playing Mississippi in their rec room.

BRIAN DILLON: Gilles had his Porsche Targa and Wayne had his Corvette in the driveway, so it was quite something back in that era. We would play street hockey right in front of the house. One of the neighbourhood kids was Behn Wilson. He lived around the corner from us, but he was younger. He wasn't the tough bastard he ended up

turning into. I played against him when he was
in Ottawa. God, for probably five years he was
the toughest son of a bitch in the NHL. Tiger
Williams was scared shitless of him. To this day,
friends that we run into, they always mention
Gilles, Wayne, myself and Gary, playing hockey
on the road. "We were in awe to see superstars and
their cars."

That is not to say the new deal turned me into a saint. If anything, that year with the Toros is what really grew the legend of
Gratoony the Loony.

One time, I got so drunk at a party that I woke up with two
girls in bed with me, and no memory of getting them there. I
really didn't know where I was, and I sure didn't know where my
car was. Looking at the time and realizing I'd better hurry, I took
a cab to practice. I gave the PR man my keys and said, "Find my
car." I have no idea how he found it, but he did; I guess yellow
Porches stand out.

Henderson and Mahovlich may have helped the team on the
ice a bit, but in reality, they were outsiders and hadn't lived the
wacky WHA road from Ottawa to Toronto like the core of the
team had. Both were class guys, but I can't say we became buddies
or anything. Remember, I was still only 22, and they were much
older.

Mahovlich always had a reputation as a gentleman and a
credit to humanity, which made him a good choice to become a
member of the Canadian Senate years later. But I was also witness
to Frank's breaking point. We were playing in Baltimore against
the short-lived Baltimore Blades, and the Big M was starting to

get loose for a breakaway. The last-chance Blade desperately tried to break his stick on Frank's back. Mahovlich just left the puck there, turned around and broke his stick on the guy's shoulder, then beat the shit out of him. I'd never seen Mahovlich act like that before. The refereeing was so bad—bush league bad.

Frank was definitely at the end of the line, though. While he could still perform decently, he was already 36 so not always tuned into the game.

> **LES BINKLEY:** We're killing a penalty and Frank's out there and he's waving his stick at centre ice. We come back into the room and said, "Frank, we couldn't get the puck to you because we were short-handed and the play was in our end."

Farda never made much of an impression, on me or on hockey in North America, but Nedomansky was another story. He was a good guy, cultured, so he stood out—kind of like me. When the great French singer Charles Aznavour played Toronto's Massey Hall, "Ned" and his wife went with me and my sister-in-law Robin, who had driven up from Buffalo.

For the second season, the Toros only played at Maple Leaf Gardens, which was a step up from Varsity Arena. But for all the romanticizing that people do of old arenas, it wasn't exactly a palace. Since we were secondary tenants, Harold Ballard made Bassett pay for a dressing room, and even then it was shoehorned near the place where the Zamboni came out. Even the washer and dryer for our uniforms were crammed into the room.

Rosters had expanded through the years, as had the size of the players. When I wasn't in net, there was a seat for the backup just up

from the bench, in the stands
with the fans, beside the
walkway back to the dressing
rooms. To pass the time, I'd
talk with the fans. One of
the regulars was a young man
named David Lively. On a
couple of occasions, I asked
him to score me something
from the concessions. But
I'd have to be careful so Billy
Harris didn't catch me—I
never did get fined.

DAVID LIVELY, FAN:
At the end of the first
period, he gave me a
five-dollar bill. Just as
they were starting to
come back off the ice,
he says, "Dave, when

Wherever I went, I would find a piano
to play. *International Hockey Archives*

we start to come back, go get me a hot dog and a
Coke, a big large one." In those days, you could
get that for that. I came back and was sitting there
with it. I go to pass it to Gilles, and he goes, "No.
no, no, just wait! If Billy catches me eating on the
bench again, he'll fine me big time." I was sitting
to the left of the bench and when play went down
to the right, he reached over, grabbed the hot
dog and stuck it under his mask. Now, when play

comes back down the other end, he hides it. And when it goes back down again to the other end of the ice, he puts his head down, quickly takes a bite of the hot dog and puts it back underneath his mask again. He says, "I need a drink." I said, "Well, here." "No, no, you just hold it. Just put it up here. Yeah, yeah. Right there." As it goes down the ice, he leans over, takes a big sip from it, and then I'm still there holding the drink as if it was my drink. It was comical.

Later in the season we had a three-man rotation in net. I still played the bulk of the games—53 total—and the ancient Bink, who was on his last legs, and a newcomer, Jim Shaw, played the rest. Jim was a rookie, even though he was seven years older than I was, having gone to university and then played in the Western and American Hockey Leagues. We called Jim "the Drug Man" because he was a pharmacist by training and had a part-time job. He was a quiet guy, didn't make any waves.

The promotions team for the Toros sure tried what they could to entice fans and draw attention to the team. The marketing slogan was "The Toronto Toros. Good Hockey. Good Fun." And one ad vowed, "We not only came to play, we came to stay." The Friday night games in particular were real party nights, with lots of young fans, and the Toros catered to them—high school groups got their names on the scoreboard, and there were cheerleading contests. It seemed there was always some promotion going on.

PETE McASKILE, TOROS TICKET SALES AND PROMOTION: We did a lot of grassroots. One of the things that we did was work hard with minor hockey associations and groups, and pushed hard, especially in tickets, for people who could never have gone to the Gardens . . . Then we started with CHUM, and started a CHUM shootout. Two young kids would shoot against one of our goalies.

At intermission, they'd have me or Bink stay out for a penalty shot by a fan who won a CHUM radio contest. Usually it was a kid, but not always. If it was a kid, then I'd be extra theatrical, putting on a show but giving up the goal. It was all in good fun.

The most famous of the Toros promos was the time famed motorcycle stuntman Evel Knievel—who had claimed that he had played hockey in the lower minor leagues, but that wasn't true—was set up for a shootout between periods.

PETE McASKILE: We made a call through ABC's *Wide World of Sports*, who had done the Snake River fiasco, and got a number for him. I called. "Here's what we want to do. We want to have a shootout on national television, and ABC says they'll cover it." And it was the same idea, a certain number of shots, and I think he got $5,000 for any one he scored. They interviewed Evel before every shot and he'd say what he was going to try to do.

I don't remember the circumstances, but I wasn't in net for that one.

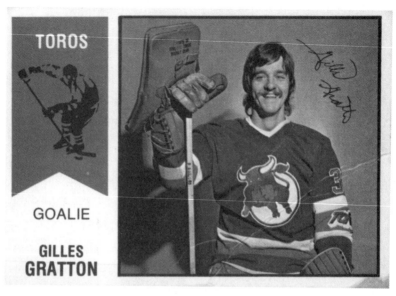

This card always makes me smile—just what am I looking at?

LES BINKLEY: Gilles was supposed to play, and I don't know what happened. Gilley didn't seem to be around that night when he was supposed to do this, so they put me in. I wasn't 100 per cent either. It's funny, Evel was really a nice guy.

Evel scored twice, at $5,000 a goal, and Binkley stopped him twice. Another time in a promo, Binkley faced a 12-year-old kid who was playing minor-league hockey in town but was originally from Brantford, Ontario. Yes, Bink stopped Wayne Gretzky cold.

Since we're talking about legends, it's time to credit two sportswriting legends who really put me out there as a character worth writing about, and set the table for the New York media really boosting the whole "Gratoony the Loony" storyline a couple of years later.

In 1974, Jim Coleman was a syndicated columnist and one of the most read, most trusted names in Canada in all of sports, not just hockey. Being 22 and from Quebec, I really didn't have a sense of who or how important he was, though he had been with us on the WHA trip to the USSR in September (I'll get to that trip later).

Coleman began buddying up to me on a flight from Chicago to Phoenix in late November. In those days, we flew coach, along with regular passengers—it was nothing like the sleek private jets teams have today. Coleman detailed my reaction to Billy telling me I'd be in goal.

> *Shortly after the airplane had passed over the state line into mountainous Colorado, Coach Billy Harris casually told Gilles that he had been nominated to guard the Toros' net against the Phoenix Road-Runners, in a game scheduled to begin at eight o'clock that evening.*
>
> *Gratton's reactions to Harris's revelation couldn't be described as instantaneous. The plane kept flying southwest at approximately 500 miles-per-hour for 15 or 20 minutes before Gilles went into his act.*
>
> *As the 727 flew closer and closer to Arizona, Gilles began to slump lower and lower in his seat until his chin was on a level with his navel. Then, he clutched his belly and, when he had attracted an audience of interested team-mates, he rolled his eyes and began to emit groans of anguish.*

A Toronto sportscaster, who had been studying the centrefold in Playboy, *looked across concernedly at the goalie, whose long thin, mustachioed face was stretched over its bone-structure like a piece of Egyptian parchment.*

"Oooo," moaned Gilles, swivelling his eyes towards the sportscaster. "I have a time bomb in my stomach. My ulcer is getting ready to explode—and it will blow me to pieces. I never should have signed a contract to play this year. In fact, I never even should have signed a contract to play junior hockey for Oshawa. Tell the captain to have an ambulance meet the plane when we land at Phoenix. This is the end!"

The sportscaster looked at Gratton curiously for a long minute and then returned his gaze to the centrefold of Playboy.

Deprived of his most attentive audience, Gilles stopped groaning. However, he staggered wanly from the airplane upon arrival in Phoenix and ate his pre-game steak without apparent relish. He failed to cheer up in the bus, en route to the rink, even when a team-mate loudly told a particularly funny story about a travelling-salesman who, overtaken by a storm, was forced to share a double bed with an elderly Arkansas farmer.

But his ulcer didn't explode like a time-bomb in the Phoenix Coliseum on Friday night. Gilles didn't even have a nervous breakdown—despite the fact that he goofed ignominiously on one of the very first shots on the Road-Runners fired on his net.

The Toros were outshot 42-to-27, but Gratton kept them in the game with his kooky brilliance. And after it was over, Gilles was ebulliently loquacious—noisy, carefree and even a bit cocky.

Historically, goaltenders have been the lonely oddballs of hockey. Gilles Gratton displays all the classic symptoms of goaltending paranoia. However, there is a suspicion that, in his case, it is a magnificent put-on.

He's like a professional wrestler playing his theatrical role 24 hours a day. He's a natural clown and practical joker, he's an accomplished self-taught musician; and he can be one hell of a professional hockey goaltender if he concentrates all his considerable energies on that particular facet of his mercurial personality.

Even reading that now, it doesn't feel like me. I'm not saying that it wasn't, it's just that it seems like a different person than who I am today.

And I can't think of any plane trip without laughing at what I used to do. The stewardess would come by, asking me what I'd like to drink and I'd have my cock sticking out. Usually a male attendant would serve me from then on.

I do want to make the point that the things we did in the '70s, like taking my dick out on a plane, if I did that today, the police would be waiting for me at the airport. It was a more permissive time. It all started with 9/11, as our rights started being taken away, and not just at the airport. A good example is John Lennon's "Run for your Life," which is basically him telling a girl that he is going to kill her if he sees her again with another man.

You couldn't write that today, and you certainly couldn't get away with the shit we did.

After Phoenix, we went to San Diego, where I opened my big mouth. After we won 3–1 over the Mariners on December 1, I was interviewed at centre ice as the game's first star. "San Diego is a beautiful city. It's too bad it doesn't have a hockey team," is what I said over the public address system in the San Diego Arena. The fans started booing me and throwing stuff on the ice. I just skated off.

When we returned to San Diego in mid-January, the Mariners and their fans were fired up. They beat us 6–4, with four goals in the first half of the second period. The fans kept chanting, "We want Binkley," and got their wish when he went in for the third.

The quirkiness wasn't a conscious thing on my part; I was just being me. But the press had noticed, which made it okay for teammates to talk about me.

GAVIN KIRK: It was our third year at Maple Leafs Gardens. He got a shot just inside his ribs, between his arm and his body, the puck hit him there. He went down and the trainer came out— Larry Ashley, God rest his soul. Gilley said, "I'm really bad here. Take me in." So they took him into dressing room of the Gardens. An orthopedic surgeon came out and said, "Gilley, what's wrong?" He said, "Well, I got the puck right there, and that's where in my earlier life I got stabbed by a Spaniard with a sword. That's why it hurts so much." The orthopedic surgeon said, "Gilley, I think you've got the wrong doctor here."

JEFF JACQUES, RIGHT WING: In the dressing room, he would count the days—hours, minutes, even seconds out loud to the end of that season, and then talk about Florida. This was pretty much to himself. I think it was his way to attempt to relax and deal with hockey and life's pressures.

RICK SENTES: Okay, is he spaced in or spaced out? Just in general, he'd just be gone and then all of a sudden he'd wake up or seem to wake up. "Okay, let's play, I'm ready, I'm focused." That was how he was getting himself up for games. He was getting into his zone. It was something that I don't think any of us had ever really experienced or been associated with.

The truth is that I was hiding something. That despair over the meaninglessness of life I felt as a child had returned. What really stands out was one night when I was first star at Maple Leaf Gardens. Here I was with a Porsche, a $100,000-a-year salary, and I sat in the car at the end of the game. All the pretending, all the pretenses that I'd put up about caring about the game just disappeared. I was back to being five years old and anguished about life. It was a kind of nervous breakdown. I sat there in the parking lot for at least an hour. The mental structure or armour that I had built up to give everyone the impression that I cared crumbled that night.

I still have no idea what the trigger was. I had fooled myself up to that point, giving importance to things that didn't really mean anything. The game of life had taken me over. Maybe it had

Bobby Hull of the Winnipeg Jets was always tough to face, even
when he wasn't having a lightsaber battle with Rick Cunningham.
International Hockey Archives

something to do with Russia, because what I saw over there when
I played for Team Canada in 1974 was troubling. I talked to people
there. It was not an easy life for them. "Why do they live like that,
and I get to live like this?" Compared to what I'd experienced in
Russia, my life felt empty, like it meant nothing despite the wealth
and fame.

I knew there was something wrong, so I sought out help. The
Toros referred me to the doctor who was on hand at that particular moment—and he was a dentist! He just told me that I was
going to be like that for the rest of my life and there was nothing

I could do about it. It would still be many years until sports psychologists were an accepted part of the athlete's world.

My old enemy had come back to haunt me, and I entered a state where winning and losing did not matter. Nothing seemed important to me. I could not fool myself to re-enter the game of life.

The departure of Billy Harris as coach put me over the edge, and my life spiralled into a kind of hell. On January 11, the press reported that he was taking a two-week leave of absence to think about things, and to take care of his wife, Sylvia, who was sick in the hospital. His six-year-old daughter, Patty, faced surgery too. He'd always been a family guy, commuting from Toronto to Ottawa for much of that season with the Nationals.

Harris came in the dressing room and mentioned, sort of in passing, that he'd been fired. We knew his wife had not been healthy. Amodeo and I both were crying. We'd been with him for three years. And then I got really pissed off.

> **TOM MARTIN:** I think when Billy Harris left the
> team, that hurt him, because he was really close
> to Billy. I think they had a special relationship,
> not only on the ice but off the ice. As a young
> player, Billy really helped him. Let's face it, Billy
> played in the NHL a lot of years and understood
> what the pressures were for a young kid coming
> up. "Don't get caught up in it." Billy liked him
> because he was loose. "Don't let the pressure kill
> you." I think as a goaltender, it would be worse.

This is a pretty good example of the relationship I had with Billy: I broke the curfew once in Winnipeg. It was about three in the morning when I was coming in with my girl. The elevator opened up and Coach Harris was standing there. He looked at me and started to whistle. No one said a word on the elevator.

It's also a good example of one of life's regrets. I still think about what an ungrateful person I was with that girl—I can't even remember her name. Every time I was in Winnipeg, she would stay with me for five days in the motel room. We'd have wine and cheese, bread, it was like a five-day vacation. She was really nice. Every time I went to Winnipeg, she was waiting for me. She never asked anything of me. I don't know why I never took her out shopping to buy her something. Nothing. What an idiot I was. She was good-looking, too, and I never asked for anything, not even her phone number or address. I took advantage of her.

The quiet exit was perhaps fitting for someone who'd been a solid contributor to Toronto Maple Leaf Stanley Cup teams. Billy had a way with me that made me want to play for him, and I didn't want to let him or the guys down.

That was not the case with Bobby Leduc. He had a broken leg and the team was already paying him, so he was made coach. Not exactly a great way to demonstrate to your players that you want the best for them.

> **TOM MARTIN:** It was hard for Bobby Leduc to go from being a player to being a coach, when you're with the guys as a player. It is different—him coming in as a player-coach. That's a difficult position to be put in.

I'm ashamed of this one, and in retrospect, I know that Buck Houle, as general manager, took direction from Bassett on Billy's firing. We were on the bus in Cleveland, and me and Mike Amodeo were sitting behind Buck. I got up and pissed just a little on each of his shoulders and then sat back down. Buck reached back to touch the wetness, felt it, and took out his handkerchief to clean it up. Five minutes later, I got up and did it again—just a little on each on shoulder. He really didn't notice besides wiping it up with the handkerchief. Five minutes later, I do it yet again and sit back down. Then he turned around, and scolded us both, "You guys had better stop it!" He thought we were putting water on him.

On a different occasion, Buck did try to talk to me about my attitude, but I told him to fuck off.

In Cleveland one night, after the Crusaders had moved to their huge new arena out in the suburbs, Leduc wanted me to play, but I lied and said I wasn't feeling well. Instead, I went way up into the nosebleed seats in the arena and read *Lord of the Rings*. I didn't pay attention to the game at all.

While all this was going down, my fame only increased thanks to a massive feature article on me in the *Toronto Star*'s *Weekend* magazine, titled "Grattoony: Sure all goalies are a bit crazy, but that still doesn't explain Gilles Gratton." It was written by Roy MacGregor, who the Hockey Hall of Fame has honoured with its Elmer Ferguson Memorial Award for journalism.

ROY MacGREGOR: I used to go into the Toros games, because it was easy access, there was always the odd story. I had heard a little bit about him, so my first approach would have been in a hockey dressing room—this is long before the time of the hand-held microphones or the iPhones or things like that, so you could sit and talk casually with someone, without out even mentioning a story. I start chatting with him. Just so engaging and so interesting that I knew right away there was a good story there. We started talking about when we might get together and have a coffee.

Roy mentioned that he and some friends played pickup hockey on Monday nights, and it wasn't far from where I lived. I asked if I could come out. He was surprised but said it was okay.

ROY MacGREGOR: I played with a group of people that just loved the game. He wanted to play out, of course, and that made more sense, but he couldn't let the Toros know, because that would have gone against his contract. They do sign things, like they won't go skydiving or play pickup hockey. But he was bored and he wanted to play. I told the guys that we were playing with. They didn't believe me. Lo and behold, the doors open and he walks in with his equipment. He had standard equipment to play out. I introduced him around. Nobody ever said a word, it never got into any of the papers or anything.

It became a regular thing for the remainder of the season. Often, I'd go to Roy's home first, and we'd split a joint and then go play hockey. I think it was because we became friends that I opened up to him more than I had with any other writer. Besides

popularizing the nickname Gratoony, he also told people about
my belief in previous lives:

> *While so many other players of today are busy*
> *investing their money, endorsing products, buying*
> *cattle farms, raising horses and thinking hockey,*
> *always hockey, Gratton draws astrological charts*
> *of people who interest him and writes pop music*
> *melodies that come to him. While others go to sleep at*
> *night dreaming of goals scored, fights won, and, for*
> *some of them, free women—hockey groupies—waiting*
> *outside their hotel rooms on road trips, Gratton*
> *sleeps dreaming of Spanish moors and blurred villas,*
> *of times past, uniforms and war. Sometimes he*
> *wakes screaming in pain and clammy with sweat,*
> *holding his stomach and scared for no reason. He has*
> *dreamt again he was being stabbed. Two mediums,*
> *at different times, have told him he was a Spanish*
> *soldier in another life, a soldier who died in combat.*
> *And sometimes during the day he gets violent pains*
> *in his stomach, always the same place, always exactly*
> *where he dreamt he was run through.*
>
> *All of this, and much more, has made him hockey's*
> *most curious enigma. On an on night, he's said to be*
> *as good a goaltender as there ever has been; on an off*
> *night, as bad. Billy Harris says "Gilles is probably the*
> *most talented goalkeeper in hockey . . . more potential*
> *than any of the young ones and the chance for the same*
> *success as Ken Dryden—if he wasn't so incredibly*

*different." Les Binkley, the Toros' veteran back-up
goaltender who has played for nine teams in seven
leagues in the past 20 years, agrees: "Gratton's great
right now. There's just no telling what his potential is.
He's great—and, boy, is he different."*

The timing of the MacGregor story, the end of March, was partly a preview of the Toros in the WHA playoffs. We'd had a decent year, finishing second in the Canadian Division, four points behind Quebec, with a 43–33–2 record. I won 30 and lost 20 of the 53 games I appeared in, with a 3.85 goal-against average.

But heading into the playoffs against the San Diego Mariners, I was done. Mentally, I was struggling and no one was able to help me. Physically, I felt beat up all the time, and not just from the wounds from past lives.

One story called my goaltending in the playoffs "deplorable," which wasn't inaccurate. In the opening game against San Diego, I gave up five goals in the first two periods and was benched, and we lost 5–3. They beat us again in San Diego, 7–6. Back in Toronto, we won 5–2 and 6–5. In our return to California, we lost again, 4–3.

For the sixth game, back in Toronto, Leduc approached me about playing. I said, "Fuck you, I'm not playing. You dress Binkley and the Drug Man." Then I left and went to a bar a few blocks down. I think I drank maybe 12 beers. I was playing pool and the PR man comes in. He says to me, "Shaw got hurt during the warm-up, you have to come." Though I'm fucking drunk, I go back to Maple Leaf Gardens, get dressed, and sit on the bench from the start of the second period on, and watch as we get eliminated with Bink in net, 6–4.

The day after we got eliminated by San Diego, I left for Florida. I barely said goodbye to anyone and was not there for the year-end team photo. Houle told the press that he didn't know where I was.

When I did get back to Montreal, I did an interview saying how I didn't care about hockey any longer, and I certainly didn't care about a possible lawsuit over breaching my contract for missing the fucking team picture. In the same story, Bassett said, "It's a tragedy in many ways . . . He's a tremendous athlete when he wants to be and he is a nice kid. But something had to be done."

Later in the summer, Bassett called me. He invited me to his cottage and wanted to mend our relationship. He knew how pissed off I was.

I said no.

That decision was probably the worst of my life, and that's saying something. I should have gone to his cottage. He offered an olive branch and I didn't take it. I still had four years left on my contract. That's when my career ended, really. Everything after that just went wrong—it was one nightmare after another.

CHAPTER 8

BEAT ME IN
ST. LOUIS

Most people forget that I played for the St. Louis Blues. I sincerely wish I could forget it as well. There's starting off on the wrong foot, and then there's the hole that I dug for myself right from the start.

The relationship between the WHA and NHL had settled down to the point where the leagues would at least communicate. I don't know exactly how I ended up in St. Louis, but I figure John Bassett sold me under the table to the Blues. Officially, the Sabres, who held my NHL rights, traded me for cash to St. Louis on July 3, 1975; *The Hockey News* reported that Buffalo got $150,000, and I'm certain Bassett got a similar amount. I signed a six-year contract with the Blues for $90,000 a year.

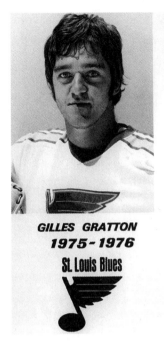

GILLES GRATTON
1975-1976
St. Louis Blues

Here is proof I actually did play in St. Louis.

The NHL Entry Draft was in Montreal that year, and the new owners wanted to meet me. Fine, it was close by at least. I got into the lobby of the hotel, and I saw Garry Young there. I knew Garry from my days in Oshawa. What I didn't know is that he was going to be announced as the coach of the St. Louis Blues. We got into an elevator and he asked me how I was doing, and I replied that I was fine.

"How do you feel coming and playing with St. Louis?"

"I don't give a fuck, as long as they pay me. Fucking hockey, I hate it."

His face went pale. On the sixth floor, he got out with me.

Five minutes later, I learn that he's my coach. I knew then that I was screwed. Sure enough, he gave me a hard time from the get-go.

One thing that helped me was that I had been in a small car accident in the summer in Montreal. I was out with a friend, and we were hit by a guy running a red light. I had a concussion, lost my sight for about half an hour, and my left leg was banged up. That was right before training camp, so I couldn't do much at camp, which is just as well. (On the subject of cars, I had given the Porsche back. It was a rental, and the company wanted to sell it to me for $7,000—and I turned it down. Another bad decision.)

The Blues needed a goaltender, because they had traded John Davidson to the New York Rangers in exchange for three rugged wingers, Ted Irvine, Jerry Butler and Bert Wilson. The other guy there was Yves Belanger, who had only come up to the Blues the season before and was hardly a proven major-league player. Eddie Johnston, who had won Stanley Cups with the Bruins, was there as the veteran backup, and the team had drafted Ed Staniowski as a goalie of the future. So I was supposed to be *the guy*.

It was just after the Philadelphia Flyers had fought, intimidated and scared their way to a second straight Cup, and the Blues still had monsters like Bob Gassoff and brothers Barclay and Bob Plager around to deal with the Broad Street Bullies. But the game was changing too, and the Flying Frenchmen in Montreal were about to take over the league.

With my long hair, beard and bad attitude, I made up my mind that I didn't want to be there. Even the city of St. Louis turned me off—I just didn't like it.

During training camp, I bailed, and headed back to Montreal. I wasn't feeling well. My leg was banged up and I was still having dizzy spells, but the fact is I didn't want to be with that team. My agent had Habs legend Boom-Boom Geoffrion get in touch. They all encouraged me to return, and I relented, briefly. On the plane, Geoffrion gave me a pep talk of sorts—odd, since he hated my brother and never played him when he was coaching in Atlanta. Geoffrion told me, "Us French Canadians, it's difficult for us. You should make us proud." I thought, "Fuck, I don't care."

Perhaps the only thing of note that happened in St. Louis for me was facing my big brother Norm for the first time in the NHL, in my debut a month into the season, on November 5, 1975. I'd faced him in junior, when he played for the Junior Canadiens and I played for Oshawa. There really wasn't anything special facing Norm. If the same thing had happened today, it would have been a bigger deal, brothers facing each other. The media would have made a story out of two brothers making millions in the NHL. But in my day, it wasn't like that at all. There was sports news at night, and that was it, and we didn't make it. But I do remember that we won 4–1 over the North Stars, and I was named the game's first star.

It's funny looking back through the game stories from my time in St. Louis. Officially, I played in six games, but in at least half of them, I left the game early, feigning some injury or other. Yeah, I put my teammates in a tough spot, but I couldn't stand the coach.

One time, on the bus, there was a flare-up when Young told me and Claude Larose not to speak French. I told him to fuck off. I roomed with Larose a couple of times. He liked to watch TV all night and fall asleep with it still playing. The first night, I couldn't sleep because the damn television was on. The second night, I got to the hotel room before he did, and I unscrewed all the parts of the television so it wouldn't work. When he came in, I pretended I was sleeping. He fiddled around at the back of the TV and fixed it up. Maybe he was a television repairman in a past life. The one guy I got along famously with in St. Louis with was Bob Gassoff, who was as tough as they come, and I suspect we would have gotten into a lot of mischief had I hung around.

My relationship with Young just deteriorated and deteriorated. It all went back to that first chance encounter on the elevator. From that moment on, I was done. It was just a matter of time.

The breaking point was during a game against the New York Islanders. Winger Bob Nystrom took a shot, which hit me in my already sore arm. I skated off the ice, partly stalling for time. I just decided I was done, and Young was forced to put Johnston in net. Coming in cold, he gave up eight goals. At practice the next day, Young accused me of letting down my teammates. Well, fuck that. I threatened to kick the shit out of him in the dressing room. The Plagers held me back while I yelled, "I'm going to kill you, you fucker!"

So I left the St. Louis Arena and went back to my apartment. I stayed there for a few days until the general manager, Dennis Ball, called me. "Let's forget about all this shit and start anew. We're leaving for a trip to Vancouver, and we want you on the plane."

"Kiss my ass," I replied.

The Blues announced that I was missing before their game on December 4, and the next day there was a supposed apology from me. Only, I had nothing to do with it. Apparently, I wanted "to make a public apology to the coach and the players for [my] conduct" and that if I "ever did play hockey again I would want to play in St. Louis, but I feel that a rest from hockey would be good. I hope that St. Louis will retain my rights on a voluntary retired basis." What a load of horseshit, just like their line that I had been out of the lineup with "an undetermined intestinal disorder."

A story by St. Louis beat writer Donald Berns in the *Hockey News* obviously had better sources: me. It talked about how I thought Young's practices were "juvenile" and that he didn't like French Canadians. This was a good line from me, referring to the Belanger/Johnston/Gratton threesome in net: "I wish we could rotate six goalies; then I'd have to play only every sixth game."

I ended up in Toronto, where I thought I could get back with the Toros. The Blues had put me initially on the NHL's retirement list, but when I got out onto the ice with the Toros, they found out (naturally) and moved me to the waiver list. That meant that I wasn't free to move where I wanted, as I had to clear NHL waivers. The Toros didn't need me, as rookie Dave Tataryn, who'd been a playing senior hockey with the Whitby Warriors of the Ontario Hockey Association, had started to come into his own. Les Binkley was still there, in his final season, as was Jim Shaw.

When I got to Toronto, the guys gave me the cold shoulder. The year before, I had let them down in the playoffs, missed the team photo, all of that. In that last month, I had just refused to play for Bob Leduc. But I did get my photo in the papers, stretching in my underwear—at least the Toronto media still liked me.

When the Toros went to Winnipeg, I went too, but I could tell it wasn't going to work. As I sat there, I told myself, "I'm not going to play for this team. As soon as I get back to Toronto, I'm leaving." Back in Toronto, I spoke with Jerry Dillon—even with three boys of his own, he still was a father figure to me. He tried to convince me to stay. I told him I was going back to Montreal and wasn't going to play anymore, and he said, "You can't do that." He was very upset. But I left anyway.

The Toros contacted me again in February when Jim Shaw quit the team, but it just never worked out for a second go-round in Toronto. The Blues played hardball, and I thought my days as a hockey player were done. I hopped in a car and drove to Florida, renting an apartment and hanging out.

If there was any vindication to be had out of the sorry state of affairs, it's that Garry Young didn't last the season either—he was fired December 14—and never coached in the NHL again.

CHAPTER 9

THE COUNT OF MANHATTAN

In March 1976, my agent called and told me that John Ferguson wanted to give me a contract, a three-year deal. He'd only just taken over as coach and GM of the New York Rangers, replacing Emile Francis mid-season, who'd been there since the dawn of time.

After all the hassles in St. Louis and the failed return to Toronto, I didn't want to play, but thought, "If I can make some money, then I can meditate, go to ashrams, do my spiritual stuff and uncover life's secrets." Like many in the 1970s, I had become interested in expanding my mind, though that had long been a part of my life anyway.

The deal was announced, and Fergie was raked over the coals in Stan Fischler's syndicated Inside Hockey column:

John Ferguson's romance with the New York press abruptly ended on March 24 when the Rangers' GM-coach signed goalie Gilles Gratton to a two-year contract.

Only five weeks earlier on February 20, Ferguson specifically was asked if the Rangers were considering signing Gratton. "There's nothing to the rumor we're going to sign him," said Fergie. "It's just newspaper talk." And so another credibility gap is opened on Broadway.

As for me, I promptly did nothing at all to get ready for the 1976–77 season as a Ranger. That summer I followed my usual routine: hanging out, having fun.

Since the Madison Square Garden Corporation owned both the Rangers and the New York Knicks of the NBA, the two teams shared offices and goofy publicity stunts. In August, Ferguson and Eddie Donovan, his basketball counterpart, had to take calls from fans for a full day. The teams had put an ad in the newspaper, encouraging fans to call and talk directly to the GMs. The goal was to sell more season tickets, but many fans just wanted to vent—475 called about the Rangers, 378 about the Knicks. One fan called me a flake and chastised Fergie for signing me. His response? "I don't believe he's a flake. Sure, he does his own thing, but I'm only interested in knowing if he can stop the puck."

Then, just as training camp was about to open, Ferguson revealed his changes to the Rangers uniforms. Talk about sacrilege. You'd have thought he had pushed old ladies down the stairs and laughed about it for all the grief he took for the first changes to the team's uniform in 51 years.

The fans in New York were something else.
International Hockey Archives

The redesign wasn't *that* radical. He got rid of the word R-A-N-G-E-R-S that had run diagonally, shoulder-to-hip, replacing it with the club's crest, and the stripes on the shoulders were bigger.

Training camp, held in Long Beach, on Long Island, was a crowded place if you were a goalie. The number one goalie was John Davidson, which was ironic, since the Blues had sent him to New York to make room for me. I'd have to say that Davidson was the best partner I had as a goaltender, and I liked him a lot. He was so friendly and positive, and at 6-foot-3, he certainly was a good example of how goaltenders were getting bigger, that's for sure. Doug Soetaert had played a few games in the previous season, and was seen as a goalie of the future, even if I was only a couple of years older than he was. Veteran Dunc Wilson was on his last legs, and would end up in Pittsburgh in a couple of weeks.

There was a lot of getting to know each other. With the Rangers failing so badly the previous year, finishing last in the Patrick Division, 15 points behind the Atlanta Flames, Ferguson set out to remake the team after he took over in January. He'd been one of the first true policemen in the NHL, whose main job was to stick up for his more skilled teammates on the Canadiens. And he was good at his job. He believed in the philosophy that if you were hit, you had to hit back, harder.

The team was in a major transition. Francis had traded Brad Park and Jean Ratelle for Phil Esposito and Carol Vadnais, and goalie Eddie Giacomin had been dispatched to waivers. Lots of rookies and youngsters got opportunities with those restructured Rangers, like Don Murdoch, and our young defense corps with Mike McEwen, Dave Maloney and Ron Greschner.

(A quick, funny story about Brad Park. Early in the season, on Saturday, October 17, we were in Montreal; we lost 7–4. I was interviewed between periods on *La Soirée du hockey*, and the announcer asked me, "How does it feel to have Brad Park play in front of you?" I went blank. Is Brad Park playing for us? What is he talking about? The guy went red, because Brad Park had been traded to Boston. It was an awkward moment.)

What I noticed in training camp and exhibition games is that my game was not on, everything was off. My reflexes weren't there. I hadn't played in almost a full year. I was out of shape. I could tell that I was far behind everyone else, but I didn't tell anyone.

I also realized that this was going to be a far different experience. My time with the Nationals and the Toros didn't prepare me for the Rangers. In Ottawa and Toronto, all the guys were decent and we got along. In New York, it was different. Head of the class was our captain, Phil Esposito.

We were playing an exhibition game in Providence and an Italian fan came in the room. There were about three of us left after the game. The guy goes up to Espo and starts speaking Italian to him. Esposito says, "I don't fucking speak Italian." He turns to the trainer and says, "Get that fucking guy out of here." In the four years that I had played pro, all the guys that I had played with were pretty nice to people. I was taken aback—holy shit. Mentally, it prepared me for an inevitable run-in with Phil.

While I liked Ferguson and had certainly followed him when he was with Montreal, he wasn't much of a coach. When the year started, he came in with a package of copied pages about an inch think. Tactics and strategies. We each got a copy. "You guys read that." I threw mine in the garbage.

Our practices were basically two-on-ones, three-on-ones, three-on-twos, shoot on the goalies. Zero strategy. If we got stuck in our end, we would stay there forever. The guys didn't know where to go on the ice. We had a young defence corps, besides Carol Vadnais and Doug Jarrett, there were guys like Maloney and Greschner, McEwen. Nobody was teaching. Even the assistant coach, Jean-Guy Talbot, he wasn't teaching anybody anything. The guys were all over the ice. I used to make fun of Jean-Guy. He'd come in the room and say, "Come on, youse guy," instead of, "Come on you guys." I would imitate his very strong accent. The guys would laugh and laugh, and Talbot hated me. In practice, he was always shooting for my head.

> **PAT HICKEY:** John Ferguson made it tough on everybody. The bottom line was, quitting was not an option. Yet he made it so tough, lots of guys would quit . . . I think in a way, he was an anti–Billy Harris, who took time for you, sat and had a coffee or a beer, but he got to know your personality and actually supported it and actually could have a dialogue about your interests in life, where you were with your life, your wife, your career. He understood everything is in development, and I think that's where Gilles played his best hockey.

Ferguson, like most coaches at the time, had no clue about goaltending. In Dick Irvin's book *In the Crease: Goaltenders Look at Life in the NHL,* J.D., who called me "Jingle Bells," described Ferguson's decision-making process as to who started:

> **JOHN DAVIDSON, GOALTENDER:** Fergie would come into the dressing room about 6:30 for a 7:30 game and he'd have a puck in his hand. He'd throw the puck to me, which meant I'd be playing, or he'd throw it to Jingle Bells. If he threw it to

me, Gratton would jump up and down and start yelling, "Yeah, yeah, yeah!" and dance around the room. But if Fergie threw the puck to Gilles, he'd walk to the middle of the locker room and collapse on the floor, pretending he had fainted.

The city was an issue for me. As a place to play, New York was not intimidating like Toronto or Montreal. In those cities, everyone knew you, and you had to perform. But New York City is so big, you could walk on the street and nobody knew you. Yet I hated it, it was *too* big.

When I got there, I said to myself, "This is going to be a long, long year." That's what lead me to the drug scene. I did cocaine a few times, but I smoked marijuana almost every day, to try to combat the issues that lingered from my previous concussions. I drank a lot as well.

Initially I lived with Mike McEwen in a house out on Long Island, where most of the Rangers with families lived. The practice facility for the team was nearby too. At training camp, McEwen wasn't told until the final day that he had made the team, and he scrambled to find a roommate; I didn't have one, so it worked out. We became good friends, even if I wasn't the easiest guy to live with.

MIKE McEWEN: He was easy to get along with. He was funny. I bought a huge stereo and I was into Electric Light Orchestra. I played "Evil Woman" for him, and he went up to the piano and played it back for me first time he heard it. We'd have practice at 10:30, so I'd wake up at 9. But at 8, 8:30

in the morning, he'd frickin' be playing the piano
and wake me up. But it was good stuff to wake
up to; he played a lot of classical. After he played
the piano, he'd meditate and I'd have to go and
stir him and get him going. You could tell he was
really deep into it.

Bill Goldsworthy moved in with us when he came to the team
from Minnesota in November. Bill was older, so we didn't really
pal around with him, but he was a good dude, even if we didn't
see him too much, as he was out living his own life.

MIKE McEWEN: We had a big house in Atlantic
Beach, with four bedrooms. They must have made
porn in there before, because it was all purples
and pinks. A couple of the bedrooms were done
up in comic strip wallpaper. It was a pretty loud
house, all modern furniture, leather and glass. In
the winter months, it was real cheap. We had it
for $500 a month, and in the summer, it goes for
three grand a month.

For a while, I had a girlfriend in town. Her name was Connie
Felt, and she was New York City royalty. Her father was Irving
M. Felt, who was the main man behind the construction of the
fourth (and current) version of Madison Square Garden. The
smaller theatre, which holds up to 5,000 people, right beside
MSG was called the Felt Forum back then. Often, I'd sleep over
at her place, near 87th and Park, overlooking Central Park.

   With the traffic difficulties—a 45-minute trip often took twice that time—the Rangers would book us hotel rooms on game days right across from MSG, especially when we came home from a road game on a Saturday night for a Sunday game at home. We'd practice in the morning, then walk across the street to a hotel for a nap. It was like being on the road, except if it was a Wednesday, you could walk down to Broadway and watch a matinee instead of soap operas in your room. Fergie's secretary had the connections, and they'd be super seats too, like seventh row, centre, or in the loge, looking down on the whole show.

But because of my lifestyle, I often found myself crashing at Rod Gilbert's place in Manhattan. It wasn't long before I moved in with him so that I could party more. It was a typical New York townhouse, a thin house with five floors. The rest is sort of a blur, so a lot of these stories are no doubt out of order.

ROD GILBERT, RIGHT WING: I had a huge five-storey townhouse on 80th and Lexington. I welcomed him in my home for the remainder of the season, a couple of months. Then we travelled to practice together. We developed this friendship. We went to Il Vagabondo, restaurants together. We had a lot of fun.

Playing his last season of a storied career, Gilbert was an iconic figure around New York City. I often wondered what he was like when he was a young player, because he's in the Hall of Fame for a reason. The Rod Gilbert I got to know lived to have a good time and held court after games at Il Vagabondo, where he taught us all to play bocce. Mondays were a regular thing at Il Vagabondo, and Rod would have a half-dozen teammates and then all these businessmen that he'd met through the years. We'd eat and then go out on the town for an interesting night.

> **GAVIN KIRK:** Rod took me around in the heydays of Studio 54. We went to Andy Warhol's place for a party, we went to Candice Bergen's place for a party. It was unbelievable.

Rod introduced me to the New York City lifestyle, which included a whole lot that can't be repeated here. We'd meet celebrities when we were out, and we were a part of the scene. As cool as it was to meet these big names, it was equally thrilling to be recognized by them as the goalie for the Rangers.

Any event that we went to, I had always smoked up beforehand. It loosened me up. We went to see Muhammad Ali in the fall of 1976 at Yankee Stadium. It was kind of boring. He rope-a-doped Ken Norton. The whole night he just took the punches on the ropes. I can't believe he won. Norton just punched away all night.

I was a baseball fan, and the Red Sox were my team growing up. That's the team that was on television at home. Now I'm a Red Sox and Blue Jays fan; if the Red Sox are in first, I'm a Red Sox fan, but if the Blue Jays are in first, I'm a Blue Jays fan. We went to a World Series—the most boring World Series game of all time. It was Cincinnati against the Yankees, October 16. The Yankees were never in it. It was ridiculous. The Reds won 5–1.

Because the Rangers were owned by the Madison Square Garden Corporation, there were always tickets around for events at the arena. I saw the Beach Boys, Paul McCartney and Wings—though for that one, I stayed for maybe five minutes and left because I couldn't stand the music. The best shows I saw were

John Denver, funnily enough, and ELO. That wasn't a double bill, if you're wondering.

One time the Eagles were performing on Long Island, and we went into their suite before the show. That was because of Rod Gilbert again. We met the Eagles, and had some of their food and booze. Then we watched the show, for free. A little while later, a bunch of the Eagles came to a game. After the game, we went down to the restaurant at Madison Square Garden with them. I'd already done my post-game smoke-up in the van, so I was high. It was surreal sitting there talking with Don Henley and Glenn Frey.

A Halloween party at Rod's place in 1976 has lived on in infamy. It was open to all the players, the coaches and their wives. While I think I know who did it, I can't say for sure, but someone brought in a cake that had been laced with hash. Most of the players knew about it, but the wives certainly didn't and especially not the coaches. I was playing the piano, and one player's wife was sitting by the piano, going "Please . . . play . . ." And I'm playing, and she keeps going, "Please . . . play . . ." never finishing her sentence. She was stoned and didn't know it. Fergie and Talbot were just out of their heads, higher than a kite. Fergie was even dancing—I'd never seen him be so friendly or smile so much.

That party is also where I got the nickname "Count."

PAT HICKEY: We were at the age where, I think we all outdid ourselves, and he got dressed up as a count and performed. I remember him playing the piano.

ROD GILBERT: You know how talented he was? He liked this album by André Gagnon, a pianist.

The album was called *Neiges*, like snow. I had a piano in my townhouse, and he could play the entire album and you'd think it was the album playing. He had memorized the whole damn album, every song. He used to entertain us with the piano. Then he could play the guitar. I guess he toyed with the music. He had a true, true gift when it came to music. Obviously, he had a true gift for goaltending, because when he wanted to play, he was unbeatable. But then when he didn't want to play, he felt that the people were stoning him, which he had done to sinners [in a past life].

DAN BOUCHARD: He had his music. He would be at practice and I'd talk to him. "I think I'm going to go there and get a little music going. They have a piano bar and they let me play." He was a New York Ranger, but he wanted to be more famous as a musician. If he had his mind right on, you couldn't put a BB behind him. That was his enemy: he could not block everything.

There were many private clubs around town, and being a Ranger got you in. There was a high-end brothel that a bunch of us went to in New York. You paid with MasterCard, and I remember that it cost exactly $75, but you had to tip the girls with cash. There was a swimming pool and naked ladies all around. You sat around and had a drink. The ladies came by to chat and eventually you picked one, went in the back, and got a blow job. I picked out a Jamaican girl. After that, we were into a whirlpool. There were four of us. I picked a different girl then. Later I went back for another blow job. It was a good day.

On the road, we were just like any other team, though the Rangers certainly had a little more money to spend than the Nationals or Toros. You never worried about your paycheque. We'd try to find a gym to play racquetball, and backgammon was a fun way to pass the time. For the record, when I left New York, Ron Greschner owed me for backgammon losses, and he still owes me $300.

Pranks were a necessity to stay sane through the long season, however. One time in the hotel, me and another Ranger were going to get ice, and we went out with just towels wrapped around our waists. We ran into two old ladies by the elevator, and they were shocked. Without even saying anything to each other, we dropped our towels at the same time and started to dance in front of them.

The travel was something. We almost always flew commercial, which led to some memorable, ah, smells.

MIKE McEWEN: We had been on the road for about a week and were really punchy. It was a commercial flight, early in the morning, the last night of a road trip, nobody got to bed before three, and we were drunk. We get on the plane. They put us in about six or seven rows together. The first thing almost everyone does is fall asleep. I think we were in Chicago, so it was about two and a half hours. You do things like cut guys' ties, put shaving cream on their head, or whatever. If you walked by that area, it just smelled really bad.

Guys started waking up with about 45 minutes left in the flight. We talked and it got loud, about whatever stuff happened the night before— nothing too bad, just a lot of talk and goofing on each other. It's pretty funny, everybody's laughing and it's loud. Then it gets quiet and somebody farted, and I mean it went through the whole plane. It was really bad. Everybody's quiet, and the Count goes, "Who farted?" really loud and in this voice. Everybody breaks out laughing, even a lot of the passengers.

The story doesn't end there though. About two weeks later, we're having the pre-game meal at MSG on a Sunday, and Fergie gets up and says, "I've got a letter from a lady about our flight back from Chicago." The letter detailed the noise and the goofiness of the flight, but this woman seemed fixated on the incredibly loud fart and me saying, "Who farted?" Fergie is all serious for a moment, and then he starts laughing. He crumples up the letter and says, "Don't do that again!"

I cut Fergie's tie on the plane one day and made a Dairy Queen–like crown of shaving cream on his head, and then I went back to my seat. When he woke up, he turned around and it was all still on him. He was really pissed off. The first thing he did was look at me. He said, "Count, was that you?" I said, "No way, man! It wasn't me." He goes, "If I catch that cocksucker, I'll fucking kill him!"

Rangers fans are certainly something else, so passionate, so *New York*. The Rangers booster club was a big deal and threw a couple of parties. It was a chance for us to mingle with the fans

▲ Four of the
Gratton kids in
March 1958;
I'm on the right.
▶ A rare shot
with almost
the whole
family, with
me, Claudine,
Norm and Frank
(Jacques not in
the photo), and
our parents in
front.
▼ With my mom
and dad.

▲ Here I am singing at
a party in "H-oshawa."
Courtesy Wayne Kewin

◄ General Gratton
▼ reporting for duty
and in action.
Courtesy Wayne Kewin

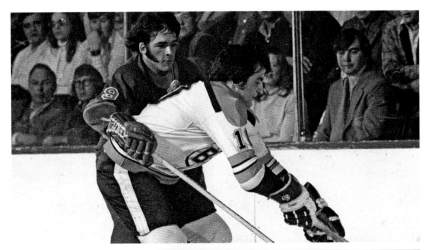

▲ My brother Norm, playing for the Sabres, tries to go around Carol Vadnais of the Bruins. *International Hockey Archives*

▶ The Atlanta Flames took Norm in the 1972 NHL expansion draft. *International Hockey Archives*

▼ With my niece Chantal Puyleart.

Playing goalie is always a bit of a scramble. *International Hockey Archives*

▲ Rick Cunningham keeps Gary Jarrett of the Cleveland Crusaders away from my
net. *Graphic Artists/Hockey Hall of Fame*

◄ My "dead fish" routine would always bring out a trainer. *International Hockey Archives*

▼ Bob Liddington of the Chicago Cougars and I both watch the puck head to the
corner. *Graphic Artists/Hockey Hall of Fame*

▲ Hanging out in our music room with my kids Charlotte and William.

◄ With my wife, Anne.

▼ My oldest daughter, Karine.

and have a good time. It's definitely a throwback to another time, as it would never happen now, the millionaires mixing with the regular folk.

At one booster party, it was set up in such a way that people would pay to be at our table. I came in to the party already stoned. I sat down and grossed out the others at my table. Eventually, I got my shit together enough to go dancing, and while I was out there, this frustrated guy comes to me, this loser, and he was more upset over the Rangers than anything else in the world. After all, the team hadn't won the Cup since 1940. He wanted to know about us even making the playoffs. I brushed him off and said, "Hey, man, I don't give a shit. I don't care. Why don't you get a life, man? What does it mean to win the Stanley Cup? It means fuck all to me." The guy was just in a state of shock. At another booster party, I was so out of it that the fans took my jacket and my shirt, and I didn't even realize it. I drove home in just my pants in the middle of winter.

The year I was with the Rangers, I got more love letters than at any other time in my life. "I'm the woman for you. I can see you're very unhappy," they'd write. And there'd be the photos too. Sometimes the love letters were 15 pages long! I'd read them and toss them out, because someone who writes me a 15-page love letter has got to be crazy!

In many ways, Gilbert and I were made for each other, even though there was a big difference in our ages. I was his willing stooge for his goofiness and pranks, and he got a great laugh. We were playing in Buffalo on January 13, and I had a toothache. Rod gave me a painkiller and said, "Take this and it'll take the pain away." I took the pill and I was stoned just out of my head—and I'm playing that night! I'm laughing throughout the game, and every time Rod Gilbert skates in front of me, he winks at me. Each time they scored on me, I laughed harder and harder. We lost 7-5. I should have let in 35 goals. I was so stoned. I don't know what he gave me.

He'd always surprise me with something. In Los Angeles, Rod says, "Let's go!" We take a cab and we get to this place and enter through the back door. It was Gino Vannelli, the musician. He was performing in town. We didn't have tickets but he found us two seats on the stage just behind the curtain to watch the show. I didn't expect it.

Once we were in Los Angeles to play the Kings, and Rod convinced me and a few of the Rangers to hop in a plane for the 45-minute flight to Las Vegas. Two limousines picked us up and we went to Paul Anka's suite for lunch. Paul sat with us, but he didn't eat. We were meeting him between his two shows. Then we went to see the second show, and we filled two tables. I remember Espo, J.D., Nick Fotiu and Don Murdoch for sure were there. After that, we flew back to L.A. That was Rod, he knew everyone.

Rod did his best to get me into hockey, but it wasn't to be. I even tried hypnosis again, and this time it was a priest who tried to get me under and really riled up about playing.

ROD GILBERT: He used to cause me to go crazy, because he said, "I'll move in with you, but I meditate 45 minutes a day, and I don't want you to interfere with that at all. If you do, then I'll move out." Then we'd have to catch a flight at Kennedy, and he'd always pick a time where we have to leave to meditate. I have nothing against meditation, but I say, "We're going to miss the plane, and I'm leaving you." He says, "Well, go ahead. I don't want to play anyway. I don't like this game." I was begging him all the time to do something he didn't want to do.

That year in New York was really something. The hockey part was certainly the bad part, but the good parts—the smoking up, the parties, the shows—were *really* good. In retrospect, it's amazing that I was high all the time, everywhere I went. One of the reasons that I smoked a lot in New York is because of my headaches. I'd have three or four major headaches each week, so I'd smoke to get rid of my headaches.

My diet wasn't exactly stellar either. On game days in New York, I'd wake up from my nap in the hotel across the street, head to the locker room, where I would eat three Big Macs, some fries, and drink 10 Cokes by the time the game started. In the warm-up, I couldn't even bend down because my belly was full. I would burp to release the pressure when the puck hit me. The 10 Cokes were to wake me up, since I was either blasé or hungover. (And I'd pee between every period for sure!)

Here's the short version of the actual Rangers season. It started out well, with an opening night win against Minnesota. Don Murdoch, the team's number one draft pick, set a team record with five goals against the North Stars on October 12. But he later hurt his ankle and only played 59 games. We never won more than three straight games, slumping in January, and then again in late February through mid-March. Davidson got hurt in December and needed knee surgery, so they needed me until his return near the end of the season.

A few moments stand out, besides all the hype I got for my lion mask. I got thrown out of a game once against Detroit. That little shithead Dennis Polonich and I got into a scuffle. I hit him and he turned around and swung his stick. He just missed my head by an inch, and I just lost it. He skated up the ice and I skated after him. I threw my stick at him, then I threw my gloves and my mask—I just fucking lost it.

A game against the Flyers in January went back and forth, and we were up 4–3 with 4:27 left. Out of nowhere, the Flyers, under coach Freddy Shero, claimed that my stick was illegal. Sure enough, the referees measured it and it was too wide. I didn't know. I was assessed a two-minute minor, and Ross Lonsberry tied the game up just after the penalty ended.

A highlight was Rod Gilbert Night at MSG, on March 9, 1977. He was honoured while still an active player, which almost never happens, and then he scored a goal and had an assist as we beat Minnesota 6–4. We finished fourth in the Patrick Division, with 29 wins, 37 losses and 14 ties, and did not qualify for the playoffs. We had a better record than two of the other teams in the Wales Conference that did qualify, though, and the league changed the rules for the following season. (Only the top two finishers in each division were in for sure, with the other spots based on merit.) I ended up playing in 41 games, with 11 wins, 18 losses, seven ties, and a 4.22 goals against average. J.D. played in 39 games (14–14–6, 3.54 GAA), Soetaert played in a dozen (3–4–1, 2.95 GAA), and Dave Tataryn played in two (1–1–0, 7.50 GAA)—more on him later.

Those 1976–77 Montreal Canadiens are often listed as the best team ever, going 60–8–12 and taking the Stanley Cup. One of their eight losses that year was to me, as I continued my penchant

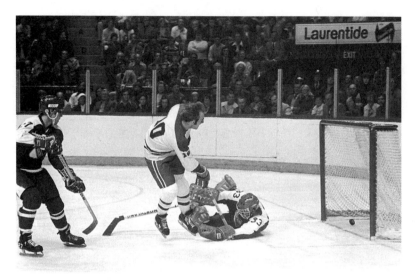

It's true that I always played well in Montreal, but here Guy
Lafleur gets one past me. *International Hockey Archives*

for playing well in Quebec. Another time, it didn't go so well.
On February 27, J.D., on his 24th birthday and only just back
from knee surgery, gave up five goals to the Habs at MSG in
two periods, and I came in for the third. The Habs scored three
more on me, including Cournoyer's second of the game. He flew
in front of the net, I tracked him as he went to the corner, and he
shot, and it went in where there might have been two inches to
score. I couldn't believe it. The fans chanted "We want Soetaert"
for a time. After, in the dressing room, a female reporter asked
me, "What happened on Cournoyer's goal?" I thought, what a
fucking stupid question. As if the seventh goal mattered in an 8–1
loss. "I let in the goal because Cournoyer's my friend," I said. It
was just a joke, and she put it in the paper that I let in the goal.

After the game, I was in a cab with Cournoyer, Serge Savard

and Rod Gilbert. I was talking about the Parti Québécois. Savard was a huge federalist. I was riling him up, talking about Quebec separating from the rest of Canada and how I would cast my vote for the PQ. The more pissed off he got, the more I turned the crank. I'm not a separatist, but I am a shit-disturber.

That Canadiens team came at you in waves, and there were no weaknesses. The NHL today is so much more even—there's parity. But that season, you had the incredible Habs and then sad-sack teams like Washington, Colorado and Detroit. You knew Montreal was going to win the Cup that year. Why don't we just give them the Cup and go to Florida early?

For me, the turning point was a battle with Esposito. There were a lot of practices where I had smoked up beforehand. I was stoned probably half the time, from October to December. But in January, when I got into a verbal fight with Esposito, I was stoned or drunk every day. Often I'd been up all night partying and smoking, and then gone straight to practice. I couldn't even stop Talbot's 14-year-old son on a breakaway.

Esposito came to me in practice and asked, "Are you playing Saturday in Toronto?"

I said, "Yes."

He said, "You're not practicing very hard."

I said, "So much talent, what can you do?"

"If you don't play well Saturday, you're going to hear from me."

Esposito was like the Michelin Man. Yeah, he was big, but he was all soft, no muscles. I was 170 pounds or so, sure, but I was wiry and tough. "You're the coach now? Fuck you. If you don't get out of my face right now, you're going to eat my stick."

He backed away, surprised. No one talked to him that way. He was the king of the team. After that, in the dressing room, he tried to suck up to me. I said, "Fuck you." I was going to go after him, but Gilbert and Goldsworthy, who were sitting beside me, held me back.

A few days later, I'm at Rod's house, and he tells me that there was a meeting with Fergie, Talbot, Espo, himself and representatives of ownership, and that it was decided that I wasn't going to play any longer. I said I didn't care.

After that, Fergie asked me to play here and there.

My excuses became wilder and wilder, and I think I'm now better known for them than my goaltending.

"Fergie, I can't play. I can't play because of a wound I suffered in the Franco-Prussian War of 1870, and my leg still hurts from that injury." Another time, I told him I had to check my astrological chart, stalling for time. Then I told him that my moon was not aligned with Jupiter and there was no way I could play because my planets were not well aligned. He looked at me and just walked out of the room.

Despite our battles, I didn't make it into Ferguson's autobiography. He did tell the *Hockey News* how he felt about me in a 1989 feature. "He told me he could see it in the stars that he shouldn't play tonight," Fergie told writer Steve Dryden. "I went absolutely bananas."

> **ROD GILBERT:** It was frustrating for me. He told me that he wasn't that impressed with the game, and he'd rather do something else. I said, "Gilles, you're making a quarter of a million dollars to play a few games." John Davidson was the number one goalie there. We were playing for a playoff spot. "You could really make the difference here when

you play, because you're better than John." He was.
But he didn't want to apply himself all the time,
and that frustrated me because I was at the end of
my career, and it was important to me.

Davidson was playing all the games, but he got hurt (again). They
called up David Tataryn from New Haven in the AHL. He'd
actually played for the Toros after I left in the WHA. He made
his debut on Rod Gilbert Night, and we snapped a losing streak.
I was supposed to play the next night in Boston, and the Bruins
were really on a hot streak.

DAVE TATARYN, GOALTENDER: We come in after
warm-ups, and Gilles goes up to Fergie, and he
says, "It's not in the stars for me to play tonight."
So, "Dave, you're in," and I go in net. That game
was—how can I say it? The bane of my existence.

That game might have been the biggest shitshow I watched and
then had to participate in. The Bruins came out roaring and were
quickly in the lead. Dave Maloney got a five-minute major for
cutting Wayne Cashman's forehead; it was clearly an accident,
despite the blood on both uniforms, but that didn't stop referee
Bob Myers from sending Maloney out. That got Fergie worked
up, and when Matti Hagman scored for the Bruins with Maloney
in the box, Fergie threw a water bottle that hit linesman Swede
Knox in the back of the head. So there's another penalty for us, a
bench minor. Another goal. When it was 5–2, Fergie got thrown
out for his constant verbal abuse of the refs. Talbot took over as
coach and put me in for the second period of our 10–3 loss.

DAVE TATARYN: I never saw the ice again because
of it, because Gilley didn't want to play the
game. It's sort of a thorn in my side—but it's not,
because Gilley's a good guy. I'm not bitter about it,
it's just that I had to move on.

That was Tataryn's last NHL game, and mine wasn't far away
either, April 4, against the Flyers. I knew I was done, and so did
most of my teammates.

ROD GILBERT: Everybody wrote their address on
a piece of paper, where we were going to be for
the summer, for the team to contact us. He wrote
Barcelona, Spain.

At the end of the year, McEwen and I drove back to Montreal.
We'd been smoking in the van. At the border, we told the guard we
were with the Rangers. He said, "Wow. My favourite player is Bill
Goldsworthy." I jumped out the van, went in the back, and took
out two Goldsworthy sticks and gave them to him. He was in a
state of shock. Before I left New York, I had convinced the trainer
to give me a bunch of used sticks—I probably had 30 with us.

After Montreal, McEwen and I drove down to Florida. We
were driving down through the Carolinas. The highways are
pretty straight there, and we'd been smoking in the van.

MIKE McEWEN: He got on the CB radio and
talked about being high and how cloudy it was
in the van. And I'm like, "Don't fucking do that!
Cops!"

At one point, I was driving and started to drift off to the side. McEwen was lying back too. Then I hear, "Count!" I jumped and woke up, still on the road. We got lucky.

From Florida, I made my planned trip to Spain and Morocco. I sent the Rangers a postcard, signed "From The Count in the Land of Love." I knew I was finished in New York, so I was just teasing them.

CHAPTER 10

BACK IN THE USSR

Many people don't realize that I was a part of Team Canada during the World Hockey Association's 1974 series against the mighty Russians. It was a sequel, of sorts, to the Summit Series of 1972. I never played a game in net, though—I was the third goalie in the lineup, behind Gerry Cheevers and Don McLeod. But I was asked to suit up for one game in Moscow—and I told them to fuck off.

It wasn't until the summer of 1976 that I tended net against the Russians, and for that game, the motley crew in front of me included students and professors from Montreal's Concordia University and a couple of pro hockey players who were also on the trip. But let's go back to the summer of 1974.

The WHA was trying to show that it was just as good as the

139

NHL, and one of its bright ideas was to take on the Big Red Machine. It was set up almost identically to '72, with the first four games in Canada and the next four in Moscow, with a couple of exhibition games in Europe squeezed in between. Three members of that '72 team—defenceman Pat Stapleton and forwards Frank Mahovlich and Summit Series hero Paul Henderson— were part of Team Canada '74.

I wasn't on the initial announced roster, but a couple of days before the training camp opened, Billy Harris called me and said, "I want you to be the third goalie on the team." Since I liked Billy, I considered it, thinking a trip to Russia would be nice. No pressure. I wasn't going to play.

But then I got to Edmonton for the training camp, and I ran into a redneck lunatic. Oilers owner Billy Hunter, who was a powerful man in the WHA, called me into the office. The conversation went something like this:

"It wasn't my idea to bring you onto this team. I hate your beard and mustache. I don't want you."

"Fuck you, asshole. I'm going back to Montreal. You can kiss my ass."

I stormed out, but Harris got to me. He said, "Wait, wait, wait. Just do it for me. I want you as an insurance policy. Just shave your beard, you can keep your mustache."

I shaved my beard and cut a bit of my hair, and I stayed. I didn't train very hard at camp because I didn't think I was going to play.

In the first two games, we tied in Quebec, 3–3, and we won in Toronto, 4–1. In the third game, in Winnipeg, I don't know why, Billy got some pressure from someone and he changed the lineup. He put McLeod in net and changed up the defense. We just got killed, 8–3. That's where we lost the series, in the third game, because we tied in Vancouver 5–5, the last game in Canada. The momentum was gone. If we would have kept the same team, the same strategy, we had them. We had four lines going 20, 25 seconds, and the Russians didn't know what to do. In the third game, they got their confidence back because we put our B team on the ice.

When Harris changed the whole lineup, there was a lot of bitching and moaning. It heightened some of the dissension that was already there. Tom Webster, for example, couldn't stand Bobby Hull—he just hated him. In the hotel one night, he invited me to the team party, but stressed that Bobby wasn't invited.

After the four games in Canada, we went to Finland for a game, and I played the first two periods and stopped 32 shots. It was 4–1 when McLeod replaced me, and it finished 8–3 for Canada. I'm not sure any of us really had any passion for the games in Finland and Sweden—it was Russia we wanted to play.

More memorable was a photo of me that made the papers. In Helsinki, I went into a sauna and a lady came to give me a drink, and a Toronto photographer took a picture. It was on the front page everywhere. Cheevers told me the next day, "My wife called me. She said she saw you naked in the front page of the newspaper." He was laughing pretty hard.

I missed the bus in Sweden because I was sleeping. I woke up and the guys were coming back from the game. My roomie in Sweden was McLeod, and he was a sleepwalker. He'd been drinking one night and I was in bed when I heard a strange noise. He was up, with his head up against the window, mumbling to himself. I got out of my bed and put him back into his. I didn't know him very well, so it was very strange.

On the bus from the Moscow airport to the hotel, I sat beside Tim Horton's widow, Lori. He'd just died the year before. She was a little drunk, and I could see all the sadness and sorrow in her as she talked to me. I did wonder what she was doing there. Somebody must have thought it would be a good idea for her to get away from North America.

On the trip, I mostly hung around with the Howe kids, Mark, Marty and Cathy; the rest of the guys on the team were too old for us—Bobby Hull, Gordie Howe and J.C. Tremblay were all over 30 years old, and there were hardly any young guys on the team. For meals, usually the French guys would sit together—Tremblay, Réjean Houle, Serge Bernier, Marc Tardif, Andre Lacroix, myself. We'd speak French.

> **MARK HOWE, DEFENCEMAN:** We all knew Gilles
> to be colourful and different from the rest, but
> that's what goalies are—a breed of their own. A
> nice young man with a pleasant, fun, casual way
> about him. Colourful dresser. Cathy even had an
> admitted "small crush" on him. She remembers
> having dinner with Mom, Dad and Gilles in
> Houston later that season, post the '74 series.

Admittedly, I had a crush on Cathy too. But mostly I was afraid of her mom. I would never have tried to do anything to upset Gordie, or especially Colleen.

Gordie died while I was writing this book. Thinking of him during that '74 series makes me smile. I roomed with him at the Royal York Hotel in Toronto. I sent my clothes to be get cleaned, and when they came back, "Grappon" was written on the paper.

I fell on top of Ralph Backstrom while playing for Team Canada. *International Hockey Archives*

Gordie came into the room, picked up my clothes and saw that. "Hey, Grappon!" Then, during the season, we're playing in Houston, the puck's up in the air and I grab it in my glove and Gordie's right behind me. He taps me on the shoulder and he whispers in my ear, "Hey Grappon, how you doing?" He was a funny guy.

When we got to Russia, Cheevers had a groin injury. Billy asked me to start the fifth game. I told him, "You know, I wasn't supposed to play, I haven't practiced. I'm not in shape. I've been drinking and having a good time, and now you're asking me to play? Now you can thank that asshole Hunter because I'm not going to play. Moscow's a pretty big city, so you're going to have to find me if you want me to play." Cheevers played hurt the last four games. He still played well.

My Team Canada jersey.
International Hockey Archives

The Russian fans couldn't get enough of Gordie Howe and Bobby Hull, and Bobby couldn't get enough attention. The Golden Jet would be outside the bus with Gordie, signing autographs. Gordie would sign for a few minutes and then get on the bus, but Bobby would stay there for 30 minutes. One day, Webster went to the bus driver and told him to just drive them back to the hotel, and he did. We left Hull on the sidewalk, signing autographs. I don't know how he got back.

There's another Howe story that still resonates with me today. During one game, Mark Howe got hit at centre ice. He was out of it. When he got up, he skated to the Russian bench. The Russians directed him to our bench. I was dressed as the backup and sitting there. Gordie was near me on the bench. I looked at him, and there was no expression on his face. Later in the game, as the play was going up the ice, Gordie held back a little, and he went after the guy who hit Mark, chopping him on the arm. The guy's arm just went limp and he skated off the ice. We didn't see him the rest of the series. His arm must have broken. You could hear it: *whap*. I knew Gordie would get him.

On the way back to Canada, we had another game in Prague, which the Czechs won 3–1. Cheevers had smartly arranged to fly right home from Russia—he teased us on the way out, saying that he was heading to the Woodbine Racetrack to place some bets—so McLeod and I split the job in Czechoslovakia. I gave up just one goal.

Overall, it was a good experience, but I wish I remember more of it. I saw a lot of the world that I might not have otherwise. I took my parents over. I don't think my dad enjoyed it that much, because he was not a travelling man. He stayed in his room quite a bit. He came to the games with my mom. My mom, who was far more outgoing, enjoyed it more.

The 1974 series doesn't get anywhere near the attention the '72 Summit Series got, and I have often wondered about that. It was great hockey, and the WHA players proved up to the challenge.

Years later, I was in a cab with Bobby Hull going to a collect-ibles show, and he started going on about the '74 series. He said, "Some guys on the team did not want us to win." I didn't under-stand what he meant, so he went on about how a lot of the players wanted to get back to the NHL, and their agents had told them to underperform while in Russia to appease the NHL. Really. Believe what you want; I certainly have a hard time believing that, but that's what he told me.

My next trip to Russia, in the summer of 1976, was one of the most memorable trips of my life, and I made plenty of friends, including Pierre Gagne, a teacher at CEGEP, the junior college system in Quebec. Pierre and his wife would become my travel-ling buddies, and he has been a confidant and sage for me ever since.

PIERRE GAGNE: We hit it off on the plane going over there. We were on the SAS plane going there, a big 747. We both rose at the same time to go to the bathroom. There was a huge Russian fellow just in front, and we cut in front of him, and both of us went inside the bathroom. Gilles used the sink and I used the toilet. When we got out, this monstrous guy with a beard and long hair looked at us, and he took us by the collar. We insulted him a little bit. Then he let us go. When we got to the Sheremetyevo Airport, that guy was waiting for us. He looked at us—he was about 6-foot-7 and about 300 pounds. A monster. He looked at us and said, "Here, you'd better behave." Gilles told him to get lost.

When I signed with the New York Rangers after the debacle in St. Louis, they sent me to Russia with Concordia University, on an 18-day trip. The idea was to compare the physical education programs of Canada and the USSR. Dr. Ed Enos was the leader of the pack, the teacher in charge; he was a dead ringer for Anthony Quinn, so we were hanging out in Moscow with Zorba the Greek.

The idea was that I would study under Vladislav Tretiak's teacher and become an even better goalie. Pffft. The day that I met Tretiak's teacher, I had a huge hangover. I'd been drinking a lot of champagne over there, because Russian champagne is very good. The meeting was held outside, and he was wearing his sweatsuit. Right from the start, he sat down with three balls and he juggled them with his legs. I was stunned. He handed me the balls, I chuckled, then handed them back and left. My time with Tretiak's teacher lasted about five minutes. That was a waste of money for the Rangers. When I got to New York's camp, John Ferguson, who I'd come to despise, asked me about it. I lied. "It was great. I learned so much."

The hockey games we did play there were totally makeshift. We used borrowed equipment, but there was still a cachet to Canadians when it came to hockey, so they wanted us to play. We did win, 4–1. I remember that. I played goal—but I don't remember who we played. That trip to Russia was just an 18-day party.

> **PIERRE GAGNE:** It was one of the best trips that I'd ever been on, because I learned a lot and I met Gilles. We had so much fun over there. He's a good musician. He did compose a song over there . . . We were all under surveillance by the Ministry of Internal Security, which is the KGB. The colonel of the KGB, he was French-speaking also. He became a friend of ours. We were six French-speaking people on the program on the trip. Gilles composed a song about him, and he really enjoyed it. Gilles can play the piano like a virtuoso.

At our hotel in Moscow, there was a piano, so each night, everybody got back late to the hotel and I'd sit and play the piano for a few hours. One night, Dr. Enos's assistant, who was an asshole, came out of his room to tell me to stop. He was angry and wanted to get physical. Curt Bennett just stepped in front of him and he cowered back to his room. Curt told me to keep playing.

I made some Russian friends. The Russian people reminded me of the French-Canadian working class—very nice people. It's the government and leaders that are idiots. When we'd be walking on the street after supper, they'd ask me to sing Beatles songs. I knew them all. They'd say, "Sing 'Yesterday,'" and I'd sing it. They were amazed that I knew all the lyrics. In those days, it was still difficult for Russians to get Western music, but they knew the Beatles.

There was an educational aspect of the trip too, and I was expected to partake. And in my own way I did—though I don't remember what we were learning, as I was drunk most of the time. A couple of times, I just lay down on the floor under the desks and slept.

That also happened when we went to a concert put on by some orchestra. I'd been drinking, and I flaked out and started to snore. Gagne elbowed me to wake me up and stop it.

Many people rave about the Bolshoi Ballet, but I remember it for a completely different reason. We had left to tour various places early in the morning. At the first place, I wanted to take a dump, and I went into the bathroom and there was no toilet paper, so I waited. At the next place, I went into the bathroom, no toilet paper. I think we hit five or six places, no toilet paper, and I'm just dying on the bus, sweating and holding it in. It felt like I was going to pass out. Finally, we get to the Bolshoi around noon, and I went into the bathroom there—and there was toilet paper!

Then there was the food.

PIERRE GAGNE: Sometimes the food was not that great. We had a small portion of steak. It was uneatable. Gilles got that in his hands and said, "What is this? It looks like a hockey puck." He threw it—we were at the Hotel Intourist, we mostly ate there. He just threw that, and it was a big room. It hit the wall and into the VIP table and into the salad of one Russian. He looked all over the place and never found who threw that piece of meat.

CHAPTER 11

IMPRISONED IN NEW HAVEN

After my summer abroad, I had a feeling deep in my bones that I was done with hockey. Training camp with the Rangers at the Nassau Arena in Long Beach, Long Island, was a nightmare. Phil Esposito, our supposed captain, never once acknowledged me or even looked my way. Some leader. And Don Murdoch was facing charges for cocaine possession, though it looked like he'd be able to play, at least.

Then I ended up in the middle of the feud between my buddy Rod Gilbert and John Ferguson, who had turned over coaching duties to Jean-Guy Talbot, but was inexplicably still in charge as GM. They just didn't like each other. Fergie had played the game with his fists, and Rod was a skilled player who would skate away from conflict on the ice. They butted heads, and Rod, after

16 years as a Ranger, left the team. He told the press that Fergie had lied to him. He also called him a moron and an egomaniac. A writer came to me and asked, "What do you think of Gilbert calling Fergie a liar?" I just agreed: "Yeah, Fergie's a liar."

The next day in the paper, there was headline with me calling Fergie a liar. Fergie called me into the office and threw the paper in front of me, and said, "What's this?" I just read the headline back to him. I could see that he wanted to punch me, like there was steam coming out of his ears.

I backed up my accusation. "You lied to me too. Last week, you said I was going to play in Philly, and I never played." He waffled, because he knew that I'd gotten him. I left the office, and next thing I knew, I'd been sent down to the Rangers' farm team, though that was hardly unexpected.

The Rangers were going to rely on the often-injured John Davidson in net and took a flier on Hardy Astrom, a Swedish goalie who had played well internationally but was in way over his head in the NHL. The team's other keepers, Doug Soetaert and Lindsay Middlebrook, who'd come in through the U.S. college ranks, were expected to be with me in New Haven. Fergie had hired my old buddy Les Binkley as a goalie coach, still a rarity at the time, but Bink ignored me for the most part; maybe he was told to from above. I thought he'd be friendlier.

In the newspapers, I played nice. "I'll go, of course I will go," I said, trying to make the best of it. "I've never been to the minors, and I consider it an experience." Fergie, however, kicked me when I was down. "He didn't give us major-league goaltending last season," Ferguson said. "You've heard the saying about someone marching to a different drummer. Well, in Gilles's case, it's a different band."

My one and only regular season game in the American Hockey League was memorable for all the wrong reasons. I was assigned as the starter for the New Haven Nighthawks on opening night of the 1977–78 season, and we were in Binghamton, New York, for the game with the debuting Dusters (they'd been the Rhode Island Reds the year before).

With my traditional Big Mac trio sitting heavy in my stomach, I reluctantly went out. My timing was long gone, and when a Duster headed down toward our end, no one close to him, I skated out to the blueline for a poke check. Whoops. I slipped, slid into the boards, and they scored an easy goal.

It didn't take long for the Rangers, and Nighthawks coach Parker MacDonald, to decide that I wasn't the future goaltender for either franchise. My main job in New Haven was encouraging the young keepers, Soetaert and Middlebrook. Fergie put me up on waivers, asking $40,000 for me. No takers. I'd heard that the asking cost was eventually dropped to $100, but that's probably bullshit. He also tried to sell me to some of the independent AHL teams, like Binghamton. Unable to get rid of me, Fergie then went and paid $12,500 for Wayne Thomas of the Toronto Maple Leafs just to have one more goalie around. Go figure.

My end came after an interview I gave to Allen Abel of the *Globe and Mail*. He travelled around with the team for a game or two, hanging out, trying to get an idea of the vibe. "It is a prison but a well-paying prison," I told Abel about being in New Haven. "I am happy to take my money and do nothing. They have to pay me for this year and next whether I play or not.

"They talk about pride and desire, but they are all hypocrites. Give a man $200,000 and he'll forget all about the Stanley Cup.

Money changes everything. I give them whatever they want from me. If they want me to go back to New York, I'll go and probably let in 15 goals. I just don't want any controversy. I want to make sure I don't breach my contract. I am at every practice right on time."

The shit hit the fan after that, and a news story featuring my quotes went out on the news wires. It spiralled from there, and the Rangers suspended me. The comment stemmed from the idea that I was sentenced to be there for a year. I'd pick up my money, sure, but it was all meant as a joke. I didn't mind the city.

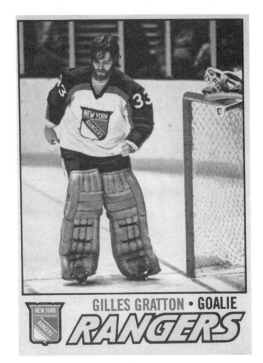

GILLES GRATTON • GOALIE
RANGERS

It seems everyone expected me to return to the Rangers; I even had a 1977–78 hockey card.

My agent in Montreal, Dave Schatia, called and started giving me shit. It felt really strange. Why isn't he on my side? So I fired him.

Rod Gilbert, who was still having his own issues with John Ferguson and the Rangers, suggested that I hire Larry Rauch, who was his agent. Rauch's office was next to Al Pacino's, so I got to have a coffee with the two of them one day. Rauch sent a Montreal-based lawyer to get my papers from Schatia; later, I questioned some of the decisions Schatia made with my money, but that's in the past; nothing I can do about it now.

Rauch's first order of business was getting me a buyout. We all sat around a table, me, Larry and John Ferguson. Fergie kept looking at me strange. "Fergie, I like you!" He didn't understand me or my desire to leave. We ended up settling for less than what the contract was, but spread out until 1981; it was important to me to have regular income.

Abel wrote another column after everything had settled. He questioned Fergie's sanity as much as mine:

> This brings us to the case of Gilles Gratton, who has been suspended without pay by New York Ranger general manager John Ferguson for "disrespectful" comments that appeared in this column a week ago. Gratton, a 25-year-old goaltender who has played only once this season for the Rangers' New Haven farm team, admitted he was not the least upset about taking the Rangers' money without having to earn it. Ferguson then fired him for telling the truth.
>
> There is a considerable difference of opinion whether Gratton, who once "streaked" a Toronto Toro practice session, is a harmless, amusing character with a loose lip or a disruptive influence on the sport he once played so well. First Ferguson signs him to a three-year contract, then he ships him out, then he suspends him for saying he likes being shipped out so he doesn't have to pay him anymore. Odd, to say the least.

There was little press when the actual news of my release was announced early in January 1978. I'd been forgotten, and I wanted to forget about hockey. It was time to head out into the world and figure out who I really was. That I had met someone to share the experience with was a bonus.

CHAPTER 12

SEEKING ENLIGHTENMENT

In the entire history of professional hockey, I'm pretty sure that I am the only one who quit the game to spend a couple of years pursuing Transcendental Meditation and yoga. I got the chance to explore my dream of becoming an enlightened being.

Along for the ride through all these years of soul searching was Ninon Prévost, who I'd met during my trip to Morocco (though she was from Montreal too). Like me, Ninon was in search of something. She'd done many different jobs but hadn't found her calling. During my one full season in New York, she'd stayed back in Montreal, and I really didn't have much to do with her—or our daughter, Karine. But after the season ended, our relationship grew, and I became a true parent. They were with me for the New Haven debacle.

FRANÇOIS GRATTON: Ninon was a quiet girl. They were travelling partners, they were spiritual partners. It was helpful to Gilles at the time. He always had his yoga friends at home, talking about yoga.

For those who don't know, Transcendental Meditation—or TM—was developed by Maharishi Mahesh Yogi in the 1950s. The idea is that you repeat a mantra continually for 20 minutes twice a day in an attempt to relax, de-stress and focus in on self-improvement. I started it in 1972 and later brought Ninon into it as well.

All the suffering I went through as a kid led to this. As a child, I would fall asleep but stay awake in my body. You're alert inside. I would go into panic mode because I couldn't move my body anymore. I would start to move my little finger, then gradually my hand, then both hands, my toes. Slowly I would wake up my body. One day I was so panicked because I was asleep that I threw myself off the bed just to wake myself up.

Even at a young age, I was reading books on astral travelling. According to the concept, the first phase of astral travelling is the body falling asleep while the mind stays awake. When I read that, I was maybe 20 years old.

One night in Ottawa when I was staying at my aunt's place, I fell asleep in my body, but my mind was still awake. Now that I was older and had read up on it, I didn't panic. I heard footsteps—it sounded like five or six people. It felt like they came in the room, and I could hear breathing. Next it felt like my bed was being lifted and these presences were shaking my bed. At that point, I was almost panic-stricken, but I forced myself to calm down. I felt my bed being put back down and they left. That probably happened a dozen times. It was the same people, the same breathing. They were very, very close to me and I felt their presence. It may sound crazy or the ravings of a schizophrenic, but it's not, and it happened often to me.

TM helped me come to terms with these experiences from my past. When I got to Transcendental Meditation academy, we started doing the *siddhis*, or programs, in the morning, the afternoon, after dinner, in the evening and before bed. Going to sleep at night brought its own rewards for me. I would wake up around four in the morning—but only my mind would wake up, not my body. I would feel energy in my feet come up my legs, and I would be thrown out of my body through the top of my head. I would exist out of my body, and I would travel.

There were many courses on TM. One was about Patanjali Sutras, and a Sutra is a like a formula that you only say in your mind. You would meditate, and after that, you would call these Sutras in your mind. Supposedly you'd get these powers. We would spent weeks in meditation, calling out these Sutras in our minds to get these powers.

One time, I was shut out of my body and I flew, and I could see all the stars, million of stars. I was travelling very fast. I landed on a planet, setting down like Superman on a street. There were buildings and people—but the people weren't the people we knew. They were very dog-like, furry and with faces like canines, yet shaped like humans. Of the three dog-people I see, one turns around and notices I'm there. He looks at me strange, as if he doesn't see me but feels a presence. When I saw him look through me, with a question in his eyes, I left and returned to my body.

The key when you are travelling outside your body is being able to will things to happen; you can fly or go through walls if you believe it, and if you don't, you won't—it's that simple. For me, what was really interesting and helpful was the meditation, and the quiet. The second-guessing, the fears, the worries, the stresses of my previous life as a hockey player just went away.

Reading Carlos Castaneda's books helped a lot. He was able to explain the concepts that I'd been struggling with, and allow my spiritual self to progress through walls and doors. What I learned from the books is that it's not a dream, because you feel like you are in a physical body, and you are in control. I learned through the books that if you will something, it happens. To prove to myself I was in control when I started to astral travel, I would make myself sit up immediately after I left my body, and slap my hands together.

When I travelled, I don't know if I was going to a different dimension or what. It seemed that the colours were more vivid. Sometimes I would recognize places, like I was at home in Montreal.

There's one time I vividly remember. I was asleep in my bed at home, and I turned to my side, and as I turned, I kept going, and when I opened my eyes, my body was going through the wall—so I was out of my body. I flew through the roof and I was up in the sky.

As I grew older, it didn't happen as often. When I was younger, especially when I was studying TM and yoga, it happened almost every night.

During all that meditation, I "burned" out a lot of shit. *Samskaras* are like impressions from past lives or this life, and these things come up and they make you uncomfortable. That's what we called burning. You feel like shit, basically. All this stuff is coming up and you're living it again, but it's being thrown out of your body in a way, out of your system. It's in you, it's your body, anything that happened in your life is recorded in your cellular memory. Let's say that you had a car accident when you're five; years later, even 30 years later, you can still feel that accident—there's an impression in your body. Usually burning is all that negative shit coming up and being thrown out of your body, which is good—but you feel like shit while it's happening. In Transcendental Meditation, they would call it unstressing. In Siddha Yoga, it was burning, or having a *kriya*, where your body could shake uncontrollably. The reaction itself is unpredictable, as some people are dealing with physical pain and others are shaking because of intense feelings of anger or sadness.

The meditation also helped me deal with all my feelings of desperation. It's hard to explain, but when I meditated, sometimes 16 hours a day, it came to a point where I would separate myself from my mind. I would witness my mind and body at work, like lying back and watching clouds travel across the sky. I came to understand that I'm not the body, nor am I the mind, I'm just the presence behind them. At some level, I knew this even as a kid. As I said earlier, today I would have been diagnosed as depressed and probably put on some drugs. But I wasn't depressed in the suicidal sense; even then I knew that we were all under a death sentence, so why kill myself when life will take care of me one of these days?

From 1979 to 1993, Ninon, Karine and I became truth-seeking nomads, rotating through four primary locations—Montreal, where we still had family; an ashram in South Fallsburg, New York; an ashram in Miami, Florida; and a couple of trips to India.

KARINE GRATTON: We were always travelling. I guess it's just something that seemed normal

to me. It wasn't something that bothered me;
I loved to travel. It was never, "Oh my God,
we have to pack again and move?" I thought it
was fun. I really did like it. I grew up into that
lifestyle. I grew up with monks at the ashram.
But there were people there from all over the
world. It was amazing—it was a part of my life
that I'll always remember, never forget. In the
real world, it's not the same. You'll never be
able to live these moments as you do when you
grow up in an ashram. Just the people that you
meet. The lifestyle. Yeah, you can joke around
and be yourself, of course, but you had to wake
up early, at five o'clock every morning. There
are certain camps that you had to do, and you
had to do work, which was called *seva*. It was
making everybody work on themselves. It's not a
lifestyle that everybody would be able to live full
time. Some would. But because it's part of my
childhood, it's also part of who I am.

Our 1982 trip to Ganeshpuri in India was important; it's different from the North American ashrams in ways that are hard to describe. It was meditation, but it was also what we call the transfer of energy from the teacher to the students, which would give you spiritual experiences. Everything about being there just seemed so much more spiritual, like the rest of the world truly didn't exist.

Of course, India presented challenges of its own. The train from Bombay to the ashram was always an experience; it would be insanely packed. On one trip, I was hanging on to a bar, one foot in the train, and my body outside the train—all the way to Bombay. Then there was a bus from the train stop to the ashram that was equally harrowing, but on a smaller scale.

In 1987, I met a Tibetan master, Jamgon Kongtrul Rinpoche, and spent some time with him. I had read so many books about Tibet when I was a kid, it seemed like destiny. My Tibetan name is Losang Dawa. In Siddha Yoga, my name is Gurudas. I met the Siddha guru Swami Muktananda in September 1979.

Of all the teachers I had, the Tibetans seemed the most authentic. I never met the famed Maharishi Mahesh Yogi, but he just seemed a nut job, charging people outrageous sums to find enlightenment. It doesn't work that way. I also studied for a bit under Sri Sri Ravi Shankar, but not for long; I found him to be a fake. Most of these guys just wanted to make money.

In Siddha Yoga, there was a guru-disciple relationship, with personal time and guidance. After the death of Swami Muktananda, Gurumayi Chidvilasananda took over as the leader of the Siddha Yoga movement. At one point, she had travelled from India to Montreal to deliver some public talks, and Ninon and I invited her to visit our home (well, my parents' home). To my surprise, she accepted. There were maybe 50 people in the house; it was jam-packed. She came for an afternoon, and we sang our Indian songs, and I played along on the piano. We also just sat on the floor and talked.

My third and final trip to India was in 1990, and I think I just felt that it would be the last time. There was not anything for me to learn there. I had hit a plateau, and hadn't found peace.

I'd gone through substantial changes through those years, however. Not that I was ever a buff athlete, but my body changed,

That's Karine on my lap as we all listen to Siddha Yoga
leader Gurumayi Chidvilasananda; Ninon is to my left.
International Hockey Archives

honed by the Siddha yoga and quieted through the peace. My
needs were few. I'd learned through meditation and yoga to go
beyond the mind to avoid suffering. To that end, from 1993 to
1995, I was with the Xeda Angels. The movement had been cham-
pioned by Marie Lise Labonté of Montreal, and the theory was
that our bodies are surrounded by energy fields, and if you concentrate on working on that energy field, you can improve your
life. Labonté channelled angels to help us do past-life regressions
and the healing of our bodies.

People often asked me about my past lives when I was playing
hockey. The most famous one had me stoning people during the
Spanish Inquisition, and my payback was becoming a goalie. Not

sure that was one I actually ever believed in—it was probably something that Rod Gilbert said one day as a joke to get his required love from the media, based on some of what I had told him.

The past lives I know about include being a sailor during the 12th century, an Indian hobo in the 14th century, a Spanish landowner in the 17th century, a Spanish priest the next, and a British surgeon in the 19th century.

The truth is that I knew about all those past lives, but it wasn't until my time with the Xeda Angels that everything became much clearer and the memories more distinct. They're just memories, they're just things that I know. I have no technique for remembering past lives. It's the same as flying out of my body: I have no technique, it just happens.

As strange as knowing about your past lives is, people are always blown away when I start talking about parallel timelines. It's difficult to explain, but I think that for every important choice you make in life there's another timeline added for the choice you did not make, like a fork in the road, and there are now two paths from that one moment. It's like the infinite universes that get written about in comic books.

While there are thousands of timelines that have happened because of the choices I made in my life, what makes me different is that I am distinctly aware of two timelines that I am currently living, and I credit my time in India, meditating 16 hours a day, for changing my body and my brain to be able to step back so that I am aware of different perceptions and see these glimpses of the other timelines that I'm living simultaneous to this one.

One has to do with Johanne, who had been a girlfriend over the years; I'd known her since I was a teenager, and she had been with me for a bit in St. Louis. She ended up moving to

Vancouver, and I haven't seen her in more than 40 years. But I have had glimpses of a life that I live with her right now. A timeline was created where I did not leave her. Sometimes when I'm doing something, like eating, this memory comes back—it's like an opening in my mind, and I see the whole scene with her. Another way to explain it would be that my memory is blocked, like a dam, and then, *bang*. For whatever reason, the dam collapses and everything floods in and I'm attuned to that timeline.

Those emotions can be devastating, overwhelming to be point of leaving me breathless, especially since my relationship with Johanne in the other timeline is complicated. I'm always leaving her but always go back—I can't live with her, and I can't live without her . . . It's that type of relationship.

The other parallel timeline I have is a little more difficult to explain. When I was 20 and playing in Ottawa, I went back to Montreal to see Louise, a friend since childhood. After I picked her up, I realized that we were totally in love. We kissed and made promises to stay together forever, raise our kids—the normal bullshit. In the back of my mind, I was going, "What the fuck is going on?" I had never been in love like that, and I'd known her for years. We went to bed together, and when I left later that night, there was a huge storm, it took me six hours to get back to Ottawa from Montreal, where it should have taken three, maximum. It was driving 20 miles an hour, and I could hardly see the road. When I got to Ottawa, I forgot the whole thing; I played my year in Ottawa and I just forgot.

About six years later, I was at my sister's in Dorion, and Louise called. She put me on the phone with Louise. When I talked to her, the memory flooded back of that night in 1972 when we were in love.

What I believe it is, and you might think I'm crazy, but when I drove back to Montreal, I think I drove into another timeline where I was in love with her. And when I came back in the storm, I was driven back into my original timeline, so I had no memory of the experience. But it's not over. The memory came back in '78, but it did not happen in this life. It must have been another timeline—but why did it come back six years later? The memory had been gone.

Then, as the years went by, I had glimpses of my life with her. I'd married her, following through on those promises that we made in Lachine, in the other timeline. I can't begin to describe just how strongly I believe in this. In one memory, we're sitting in a restaurant, and our three kids, two daughters and a son, have grown up and have left the house. She is telling me that she wants some time by herself, that we need to give each other some space. When that memory came back, so did all the emotion, all the sadness, and it was paralyzing.

In another memory, I meet her again, and she insists that we should continue to be apart. It's heartbreaking. When the memory comes back and I relive the scene, I'm sad for three days, and I can't shake it.

In our timeline, I haven't seen Louise for 45 years, but I know the life I have had with her in the other timeline.

So, as you might expect, hockey was very much an after-thought during all this soul-searching—though my agent Larry Rauch did track me down at the ashram in Miami in the winter of 1979 and told me that the Edmonton Oilers wanted me to come in for a tryout. I turned him down and told him I was not going back, ever. That was a last-ditch effort by my agent to get me back into the game. I drifted away from my friends, including people from Montreal, like my bandmates. There were new friends, ones who shared my quest for the spiritual world. One of them was Bruce Jessop, who would be my saviour when I hit a dark time in my relationship with Ninon.

Here I am with Gurumayi Chidvilasananda.

For many years, we were a happy family, and Karine was the centre of our life. Ninon and I married in 1981. Like many couples, Ninon and I started to drift apart, and tensions increased when we settled back into Montreal, our wanderlust affected by the reality of not being able to afford the trips anymore. My hockey money was all gone.

KARINE GRATTON: There weren't many issues from when I was a child growing up, but as I got a little bit older, and then my dad got a job, and we stopped going to the ashrams, I think from then on, that's when things maybe started falling apart a little bit. I have to say, when it comes to family, when it comes to caring about people that are close to you, he's the type of person that will be there, no matter what. If you need anything, whether it's listening, or you need help, no matter what it is, when it's family, he's there. He was the type of father that I was always able to count on. I'm speaking very honestly, there's not one time in my life where I can say he wasn't there for me if I needed anything.

Ninon sought out her own identity, her own career. Karine was the focus of her attention, and mine. Ninon was a master at finding little jobs—a couple of weeks here, a couple of weeks there—and would often use Karine in the process, like setting up outside a church with a camera for baptisms or confirmations. That could mean $400, $500 just that day.

KARINE GRATTON: When I was little, my mom worked as an aerobics instructor. For a few years, she stopped working. Then she went back to school. Now she is a reiki master. It's spiritual healing, basically. When they got into the meditation, it got my mom really into it. She got very interested in the whole practice—all meditation, spiritual healing. She became a very spiritual person. My dad got into it too, they both did. So my mother wanted to make that a career, which she did. When she got her degrees and everything, she opened up her own business.

Ninon and I were really into healing crystals for a while, and even went to a course in New Mexico, which Steve Dryden noted in his profile of me in the *Hockey News* in 1989. At the time, we were distributing incense, natural soaps and herbal teas imported from

India to stores across Canada. That only lasted a few months, though. From 1991 to 1995, I worked at a Costco.

I stuck with Ninon until our daughter was 20, and then I left. Karine could see that things weren't working out with me and her mom. I remember sitting down with her and saying, "I've got to go. I can't do this any more." Karine said, "That's fine."

I knew I couldn't stay close, because I knew what would happen—I would leave Ninon and come back. I'd left twice before. That was the third time. We're creatures of habit. After two weeks, I don't eat regularly, life isn't right, and so I'd go back to her. Leaving for Europe meant I wouldn't be able to come back.

CHAPTER 13

EUROPEAN VACATION

My first night in Germany, Bruce Jessop handed me a camera and said, "We're going to shoot a game tonight." Despite protesting that I'd barely used a camera in my life—especially not the kind of high-end equipment he used to shoot sports—he insisted. Groggy from the jet lag, I somehow managed to stay awake both for his instructions on using the camera and the actual hockey game, a second-division league contest in Timmendorf.

Bruce basically gave me work as a photographer from then on. He still runs a photography company and owns one of the largest hockey photo collections in the world. Most of his contracts are with the International Ice Hockey Federation, so I shot events like the World Championships in Vienna in '96 and Finland in '97, and the World Juniors at the end of '96, when the Canadians

Gilles Gratton, photographer. *International Hockey Archives*

won gold with Marc Denis in net. Plus we covered the Swiss league, the German league, the French league and the Europa Cup, which featured the best club teams from Russia, Finland, Germany, Sweden. So there I was, a guy who'd run away from hockey, being paid to photograph it.

BRUCE JESSOP: He was having a hard time in his relationship. I had put him up a couple of times in Canada. He was always in and out of

the doghouse there with his women. Because he
was a friend, I thought I'd create a position for
him. I took him out. I think the first games were
on net-cam at the World Championships in '96.
He, being a goalie, was behind the net, and I
think he had a good time doing that, making the
save. I think that worked out fairly well. Little
by little, he was able to do more, and get used
to the equipment, lenses, focus, speed, set-ups.
He became quite helpful. We had a lot of work
sorting. Those were the days of slides. You didn't
have digital files. So we used to have to frame
everything and then put them into player folders,
team by team. We were doing hockey cards in
Switzerland, doing hockey cards in Germany, the
IIHF. We also had to cover two German leagues.
That kept us pretty busy.

It made for a unique story. RDS, the all-sports channel in Quebec,
did a profile on me in Vienna. They showed me taking pictures
at a game and talked about my hockey career. All my friends saw
it back home, and for many, it was the first they had heard of me
in many years.

Of course, I was still able to talk hockey too. I met famed
Russian coach Viktor Tikhonov, and I wish I could find the photo
I took with him. Martin Brodeur and his New Jersey Devils had
won the Stanley Cup in 1995, but in 1996, the team hadn't even
made the playoffs, so there he was in Vienna, playing for Canada
at the 1996 World Championships. Since there is a brotherhood
of goalies, in a sense, I talked to him for a bit. Canada got beat by

That time I met Steffi Graf. *International Hockey Archives*

Germany 5–1, and he played terribly. He told me it was because the ice surface over there is wider and he had troubles with his angles. Canada rebounded to win a silver medal.

At the finals for the German hockey league in the spring of 1997, I was putting up the strobe lights we used, when I saw tennis star Steffi Graf. I told Bruce, and he asked me if I wanted my photo taken with her. I said I didn't care, that it wasn't a big deal to me. So he goes to Steffi and says, "My buddy wants to have his photo taken with you." She said sure. As I was standing beside her, I tried a line: "You know, I just flew from Montreal just to see you." She smiled and said, "Sure." Bruce took the photo and it ran in a German magazine, and the caption ran that she knew me from the NHL, which couldn't have been true. I will say that she seemed very unhappy, as it was around the time that her dad was in prison

Bruce Jessop and I outside our bus. *International Hockey Archives*

for tax evasion, and she was at the tail end of her career. But she was there to watch the hockey finals, between Adler Mannheim (the Eagles) and Eisbären Berlin (the Polar Bears).

In 1997, at the World Championships in Helsinki, we were staying at a nice hotel and having breakfast. Bruce disappeared for a bit, and when he returned he was urging me to come over and meet an old friend. He even claimed he couldn't remember the guy's name. I went over and was stunned. It was John Ferguson, my old Rangers coach and GM. We were both in shock for a good 30 seconds before we started to catch up a little bit. Similar encounters happened while I lived in Europe, and I know word travelled back to old friends in hockey that I had resurfaced.

I first met Bruce through Transcendental Meditation in Quebec in the spring of 1978, at the meditation academy in

Lac-Beauport. He had worked as a photographer at Canadian Press before going freelance. He was always involved in something or other, and at that time, he was teaching meditation courses. We became fast friends, and by the end of 1978, we had started a business together in Ottawa. It was called Harmony's Consumers Club. You had to be a member to get deals on stuff. It lasted maybe a year, that's it. I was not cut out to be a businessman. The business actually ended when the building burned down—we didn't have any insurance. The business was already burning down metaphorically anyway, so it didn't matter. We didn't do very well. He also convinced me to invest in his business selling satellite dishes, which went a little better—but no one got rich.

Through thick and thin, we have kept our friendship. I left Transcendental Meditation to go into Siddha Yoga, and he stayed in TM. Then I convinced him to switch over to the yoga in 1983.

Here's a story about Bruce. We were in Vienna and we were fixing the lights in the arena, me and another French-Canadian photographer, Nick Fourmier. We're walking down the stairs, and there's this girl washing the cars, Škoda cars, in each corner of the arena for the World Championships. I'm talking to Nick, but as I walk by the girl, she hears my voice and she turns around and she looks at me with a blank look. The stare lasted and lasted. I knew that I knew her from somewhere. It had to be from another life.

I started talking to her—she was about 25 and had the job part time while she was studied to be an actress—and she recognized me in her subconscious. I asked her out for lunch the next day. I wasn't attracted to her, but we had a connection. Sometimes when I meet people, I get these images in my mind; as I was having lunch with her, I saw her with Bruce in a past life. We met twice, as I wanted to make sure that I wasn't mistaken. The second time, I was convinced. I said, "I'd like you to meet a friend of mine."

The next day, I introduced Bruce to her, and eventually they got married and had two kids. I knew they were going to get married even though there was a 23-year age difference. Do you find that strange? It's like she recognized me, but then the conscious mind took over. She went blank. I recognized her right away, because I can do that.

As for my own love life, in 1997, I met a Flemish woman, Lief, in Belgium, and I managed my schedule around seeing her, trying to get back once a week.

> **BRUCE JESSOP:** Lief is sort of his ex-wife type on steroids. We lived in France in an enormous an old abbey that was partially converted, that had a church that could sit 150 people. One night, he's getting it on with his pit bull across the way, at least 60 yards away, and we hear this scream, almost like a werewolf howl. His girlfriend had convinced him to let it all out when he had an orgasm. I think it woke up half the town.

One day, Lief and I went skating. In Belgium, people rent their skates, as most don't own a pair. That means, in general, they are pretty bad skaters. While we were out there, one guy noticed what a good skater I was. We started talking, and he mentioned that he and some friends played hockey. He asked if I'd played, and I said, "Sure, I played in the NHL." It wasn't long before I was teaching hockey to about 50 people. There were women, a few kids—anybody. I was teaching skating, shooting, basic stuff. It was not difficult, because they were beginners. They were paying me 1,500 francs a month, just to teach once a week. And I had my job with Bruce too. I could do both, thanks to the great train service in Europe.

Bruce had a bus that he'd converted into a trailer that we could live in, with a kitchen, a shower, the whole works. It was great to go from location to location and drink beer all night and just shoot the shit. We'd often invite other photographers and friends to the bus after the games. Or we'd invite some girls back. The bus was parked in Vienna for a month for the World Championships, and I bet our pile of beer cans could have filled it had we not cleaned up occasionally.

In September 1997, I returned to Montreal, with a return ticket to go back to Europe just after Christmas. A lot happened during that time. For one, I officially divorced Ninon on December 11. For some extra income, I'd called my old boss at Costco, and she invited me back to work, even with the knowledge that it was short-term.

During that time, I was living with some friends in Verdun. One buddy said that he had a friend coming over that he had been trying to woo for the last two years. When she walked up the stairs and I saw her, I saw my past life with her. We talked a long time. When she left, I told my friend, "I'm going to have three kids with her." He fell out of his chair. "What?"

I was wrong. We only had two.

CHAPTER 14

A SECOND LIFE

You would never know it from the stories I've told earlier, but I am really, truly a homebody. I don't go out anymore, just to work and back. My best times are hanging out with my children.

Karine is an adult now, and I am immensely proud of her. Like her mother and I, she found her own way in life, whether it was waiting tables, doing odd jobs, selling cosmetics or working as a makeup artist. She is smart with her money and has her mother's drive.

KARINE GRATTON: I've never seen Gilles partying, I've never seen him out with the boys. For me, when I try to picture it, it's kind of weird, because I see him in a different way. I see him as a caring,

loving person, someone that's there, that will bend
over to help his family any way he can. I don't
know him as the party guy. He loves to tell a joke,
and he loves to make people laugh.

My second family was with Anne, who I met in the fall of 1997
and married in 2010. When I saw her, I knew her from a past life.
I knew it right away. People scoff at that, but it's true. And there's
more to the story.

I used to have these real vivid dreams where I would walk with
these two beings in a forest. We didn't say anything, but I felt a
closeness to these two beings. When Anne was pregnant, I had
a dream where she was giving me her breast to suckle, like I was
a little baby. The next day, I read in a book that when your wife
gives you her breast in a dream, it means that you're going to have
a boy. William was born in August 1998. When she got pregnant
with Charlotte, who was born in March 2000, I dreamed of her
about 15 times before she was born, through the years as she aged.
I told Anne that the next baby would be a girl, since I dreamed
of her many times. The Charlotte I dreamed of looks exactly like
the Charlotte I have today.

Then I came to realize that the two beings I'd walked with
in the forest in the waking dream were William and Charlotte.
After Charlotte was born, I was at peace. It was as if the missing
parts were there now. If I hadn't had my kids, I'd still be feeling
the way I felt my whole life. Unease, malaise. When they arrived,
I felt like I had fulfilled my purpose on Earth.

It's difficult for me to be away from my kids. Anne was at
home and took care of them until they started at an alternative
school at age seven. As a couple, Anne and I did not go out, so

our kids don't know what a babysitter is. Charlotte and I play a lot of music together, and she definitely has the musical talent that I was gifted with. At 14, she started taking actual lessons, since I'd already taught her all I knew. William and I play a lot of cards.

On a trip to Toronto in 2015 to work on the book and for a reunion of the Ottawa Nationals and Toronto Toros, I was really out of sync. The Toronto traffic freaked me out, which is strange considering that I used to live there—but the city had grown so much, especially compared to Montreal.

CLAUDINE CLOUTIER-GRATTON: I know Karine loves him. Gilles was a really good father and I know he still is when I look at him taking care of William and Charlotte.

Looking back, though I didn't grow up in the most loving, functional family, I learned so much about being there for each other.

For a while, Anne, the kids and I lived upstairs in my parents' home. It meant we didn't have a lot of expenses, sure, but it also meant that we were around for the worst of times.

My dad had a heart attack when he was 76, on October 17, 2001. For quite a while beforehand, he would be out of breath doing anything.

I'll tell you how my family is. When my dad died, he was in front of the house, raking the leaves, and he fell. *Pop!* They called me at work—I was working at Costco at the time. When my dad died, he fell on his back. My wife called me and said that she thought he was dead. I said, "Do you *think* he's dead? Or *is* he dead? Because I'm not going to leave work if you just *think* he's dead." She said, "No, he's dead." I told my boss and left. I got home, and there was nobody around. About 20 minutes later, my mom walked in with my oldest brother, Jacques. She said, "Well, he's dead. But at least he had time to pick up the *Journal de Montréal*."

Two things stand out from the day before he died. My mother was the one that took care of business. My dad couldn't even write a cheque, but he could read and write and sign his name. It's funny, she showed him how to write a cheque the day before he died. She says to him, "I may die one day, so I want you to write the cheque."

The night before he died, I went downstairs and we talked for about two hours. He'd never done that in his life. And he died the next morning. The autopsy showed that he had a heart attack the morning before the day of his death, so he knew he was going to die—that's why he talked to me for two hours. He didn't want to live anymore, and I know why he didn't want to live, but I didn't find out until after he died.

I also saw him twice after his death. It was connected to falling asleep in my body and getting out of my body. Since I lived upstairs, with mom and dad downstairs, I could feel that my dad was not gone. He was dead, but I could feel him when I went into the basement, when I went into the garage. I felt his presence.

One night, I was lying in bed—I wasn't asleep, but I had closed my eyes—and when I opened my eyes, I was downstairs in the living room in what I would call an energy body. It's almost a physical body. My dad was sitting in his chair.

I tell my dad, "I want to talk to you." He looked at me and he didn't really want to talk to me. I said, "Come, follow me." We went to the balcony at the front of the house. I showed him his van. He said, "Where's your car?" I had a four-year lease on Hyundai, but when my dad died, it happened that the lease was up, so I let the car go because I had my dad's van. I said to my dad,

"Well, when you died, I gave the car back to the dealer, because I have your van now." We went down from the balcony and alongside the house to the backyard, where there had been a white metal shed. He said, "Where's my shed?" I said, "I tore it down when you died." He also said, "Where's the other pine tree?" I told him I cut it down after he died too.

Then I said to him, "What happened when you died?" He said, "Well, it was dark for a bit, then I heard a voice say, 'Fernand, you're a good man. So I was not scared so much.'"

Then I remember looking up into the sky, and it's difficult to explain, but it looked like a pastel painting, an astral world, with bright colours. A vehicle came by, like a cigar-shaped bus with no wheels and no windows. There were people in the bus, waving. I turned around to look at my dad, and I felt my energy body fading away. I closed my eyes, and when I opened them, I was back in bed.

As the days went by, I could still feel his presence. One night, lying in bed, I closed my eyes, and when I opened them, I was in the basement in the energy body. My dad was sitting on the chair, and I said, "You know Dad, I love you very much, and we all love you, but I don't think it's good for you to just hang around. It's time for you to leave the house and go." He looked at me and didn't speak, but sort of nodded a yes. When I opened my eyes, I was back in bed. After that, I didn't feel his presence.

Back in 1990, I also met my granddad after he died, and it was very similar to my experiences with my dad. I was in bed, and I closed my eyes, and when I opened them, I was on a road, walking near my grandfather's home. I saw him in front of his house, on the farm. I walked up to him and began talking. He was still hanging around after his death. But what was strange was that he didn't live there at the time of his death, he had been living in the village. It was as if he had recreated his environment from when he was alive. I asked, "Have you been here a long time?" "Yes," he said, "I've lived here my whole life." It was as if he didn't want to leave the place that he'd been his whole life. It fell to me to let him know that he was dead.

After my father died, I got to know why he had lost a lot of will to live.

During the last few months of his life, I'd come home from work, I'd park my car and I'd see my dad washing the floor. Goddamn, he liked washing the floors. But why was he washing the floors so often? I remember asking Anne if she knew.

But when my Dad died, it was me washing the floors every day. The reason was that my mom could not make it to the bathroom. She would not go into an old folks' home. She was really stubborn. So, it fell to me to start cleaning up.

In 2001, at the age of 76, she just became incontinent. She kept falling down too, so I'd have to go and pick her up. One day, she fell in the bathroom on the edge of the door frame. I called an ambulance, but she didn't want it. I had a sore back and she weighed 196 pounds or so, and I couldn't lift her. It took three EMTs to get her out of there. Her sugar level had fallen to two. The one EMT said, "At two, she should be in a coma." She refused to go to the hospital, and they made her sign a bunch of papers. She ate some stuff, her sugar went up, and they left. But she fell down almost every week.

CLAUDINE CLOUTIER-GRATTON: One time, I remember, it was around 11 o'clock, and she was sick, puking. She made a mess. Gilles was so discouraged. He looked at me: "I washed all the floors yesterday." He was really a good son for his mother. It was a really sad thing, but he was always turning it funny. Let's say my mother was drinking Diet Coke, and he said to my mother, "No, Mom, no. Don't drink that. It's poison. They put that stuff, aspartame, on bodies of dead persons. If you keep drinking that, they won't have to use it, because you'll already be embalmed." My mother would laugh at him. "Hey, open my Coke." My mother was a woman who loved life. She lived to the end, I can tell you that. She was funny. She always wanted to play cards. And she was always laughing at Gilles's jokes.

Mom's illness meant I had to eventually quit my job at Costco because I couldn't manage everything. I was too tired. My brothers and sister couldn't—or wouldn't—help. Claudine lived too far away. Frank lived closer, in Dorval, but he came by one time and complained about how much it stank, and Mom got upset and took him out of the will. Norm lived in a shithole in Ville-Émard and was drinking all the time.

And Jacques? Who knows.

KARINE GRATTON: It was a difficult part of his life, because when you're seeing your mother falling apart, those are difficult moments. It's not an easy thing, and he was there for here 100 per cent from the beginning until the end. Not everybody's there for that, to help and take care of the other person. But he was there, and he very committed and

very devoted to that. I remember very well that he
was probably the only person, and she was really
lucky that he was there. My grandmother was very
stubborn. She was a beautiful, good-hearted person.
Gilles is like his mother.

Because of the diabetes, she got an infection in her foot. She was
limping and I asked her about it. She said that she just hit her foot
on the wall. She was lying—she was always lying. One day, I came
home from work and my aunt was there, and she told me that my
mom was in the hospital. She had checked my mom's foot, found
it to be infected, and called the ambulance. She never got out of
the hospital. In July she went in, and she died November 4, 2006.

We had a particularly heavy talk in the hospital, just after the
doctors told me that it was only a matter of time.

I told her, "You're going to die."

She said, "I know."

"How do you feel about it?"

"We all have to die."

One Friday she told me, "I'm going to be gone tomorrow
morning."

I spent the day with her. My brothers Frank and Norm, they
went hunting, and Jacques was doing his thing in Quebec, whatever that was. Claudine came down Friday morning but went
back home. I was left alone with my mom. Around eight p.m., I
told her I was heading home to rest and would be back later. She
was praying as I left. What my mom did a lot in the last years of
her life was pray. She always had her rosaries. Usually she never
went to church, though she went to church more in the last years
of her life.

I got a call from my aunts, who had been away in Atlantic City. We met at the hospital around 11 p.m. My mom had an oxygen mask, and she took it off. The nurse came in and asked her to keep it on. "It's bothering me, and I don't want it anymore," she said. From there, everything went downhill. As she started to drift into a coma, she held my hand. I could feel the strength in her hand initially, and at 3 a.m., her hand went limp and she was gone. Her body kept breathing, but I knew she was gone. At 7 a.m., there was a deep breath, and that was it.

During the week, I'd asked her if she was afraid. "No, I'm not afraid at all." She was pretty cool about it. I think what helped her along was the praying. Somehow it keeps your mind focused. For me, it was a good lesson on how to die. She died a good death. She died not scared, she wasn't screaming or anything. It was very peaceful. I was the only one left, which tells you what kind of family we were.

We had talked about what might happen when you die. I told her about the tunnel and light that I had read about in so many books. I told her just to go to the light. It was really the first time that she'd shown any interest in the kind of things I was interested in.

As they say, dying is easy. Living is the hard part.

Not long after she died, we moved to Montreal's South Shore, since we couldn't pay the mortgage on my parents' old home.

One of the good distractions through all this was the hockey career of my nephew, Frederic Cloutier, also a goalie. He's the son of my sister, Claudine, and her husband, Donald. They lived in La Beauce, running a maple farm. In his last year of junior, with the Shawinigan Cataractes of the QMJHL, he had 42 wins against eight losses and two ties. He won the Jacques Plante Trophy, he was on the Second All-Star Team, behind Drew MacIntyre, in Canada, and a First-Team All-star in Quebec. And he wasn't drafted.

I was working at Costco in Pointe-Claire, and I saw Jacques Lemaire, who was the coach of the Minnesota Wild at the time, in line to buy something. I knew the Lemaires, since they lived in my neighbourhood when I was growing up, but a few streets over, across the tracks. Jacques was a few years older than me, but I went to school with his brother, and, of course, we played against each other in the NHL. I said hi and found out that he was heading off to his cottage. I knew that Frederic deserved better.

"I don't want to suck up to you, but I want to talk to you about my nephew."

"What about your nephew?"

I told him all about Frederic's accomplishments.

"Wow. That's pretty good. Who drafted him?"

"Nobody."

"What?"

He took out his phone, called the Wild's chief scout, and told him to check out Frederic Cloutier. Not a day later, Frederic was offered a contract and was assigned to the ECHL team for the Minnesota Wild, the Louisiana IceGators. He played in the AHL and a couple of times he was actually in the NHL, but he never played—he just sat on the bench.

FREDERIC CLOUTIER: We lived about three hours away from Montreal. Uncle Gilles used to come every winter, Christmastime, with his oldest daughter, Karine, for Christmas, to spend school's Christmas break. I was maybe five or six years old. It was about the time when I realized

My nephew Frederic Cloutier warms up for an exhibition game with the Minnesota Wild. *International Hockey Archives*

that my Uncle Gilles actually played in the NHL. I found a picture on my parents' dresser of my uncle wearing his famous goalie mask. I remember clearly that I asked my mom, "Who's this? It's a cool picture." My mom said, "That's your Uncle Gilles. He played in the NHL for a few years, and the World Hockey Association also." Then I said, "I'll do the same thing as him when I'm older." I never had the chance to play in the NHL, but I was somehow still able to get a career out of it.

Now Frederic is in Europe, married to an Italian girl from the northern part of the country, and they have two daughters. He now speaks French, English, German and Italian. He became an Italian citizen and was a part of the country's silver medal at the 2016 IIHF World Championship Division I—the secondary teams—in Poland and Croatia. It turned out real well for him, even if he didn't have an NHL career. In Europe, as a hockey player, you don't pay rent or taxes, and the team gets you a car. Most recently, he's been in Finland.

> **FREDERIC CLOUTIER:** My uncle always told me, "If anybody ever asks you if I'm your uncle, you just say no." When I signed my contract with the Islanders, Mike Milbury was not a very big fan of my uncle's. They didn't like each other when they played against each other. He said, "I heard the rumours that Gilles Gratton is your uncle." I said, "Yeah, I'm not sure if I should tell you yes or no." He's said, "Listen, as long as you're not as crazy as he is, I think we're going to be okay."

Since summer ice time was hard to come by where Frederic lived, he used to come to Montreal and stay with his grandmother, and we were just upstairs, of course. He saw how her health deteriorated year to year.

> **CLAUDINE CLOUTIER-GRATTON:** Sometimes Frederic would phone me at night. "Oh, we had so much fun tonight." They would be on the balcony,

Frederic, Gilles and Grand-maman. "We laughed all night."

At the end of 2004, I got a call from Mark Napier, who asked if I would be interested in an NHL old-timers tour out in Western Canada. I said yes. While the trip and the experience were great, it was about the money—I got $500 a game. We started in Lethbridge and we ended up in Thunder Bay. In all, it was 10 games in 12 days. We had two vans. The guys I remember from the tour were Tiger Williams, Bryan Trottier, Mark Napier, Morris Lukowich, Bob Bourne. They were all great guys to travel with, and I learned some surprising things, like Trottier's Metis heritage and his knowledge of French. Tiger's sister lived near one of the towns, and we went there for dinner, and she spoke French because she worked with French people. We had a great time at her place, and then after that we went to a bar where there was music.

I hadn't played goal since 1977. I wore equipment that belonged to my nephew, who had a virtual storehouse of old stuff in my mom's basement.

> **FREDERIC CLOUTIER:** I remember talking to him a couple of weeks after. He couldn't believe how light the equipment was compared to what he wore. That was the early 2000s, and if you compare it to now, it's even lighter.

The good news was that I didn't have to do much in net, because the old-timers games are meant to be fun. Yet I still ended up hurting my neck and back just by moving so differently, using muscles that I hadn't used in a long, long time.

With baby Charlotte and my nephew Frederic.

That was also the first time I'd been away from my kids. Charlotte was four years old and William was six. I would talk to them on the phone every day. When I came home, I was upstairs with my mom. Charlotte got back and was shaking uncontrollably when she saw me, it was as if she thought I was dead; she didn't understand me just being away. I was so traumatized by what I'd put my kids through, I turned Napier down when he called a short time later.

Perhaps by now you've seen that hockey has a way of coming back into my life, even if I don't want it to. I went to Europe to get away from relationship issues, and ended up photographing hockey. Then there was helping Frederic out, and the old-timers tour.

But the best example of my twisted connection to the game

is Classic Auctions. It's a major auction house that specializes in sales of hockey memorabilia.

In 2005, my old buddy Bruce Jessop decided to sell his collection of primarily old jerseys to Marc Juteau, who owns Classic Auctions. While Bruce was still in Germany, all his memorabilia was in Montreal, at his mother's house. I ended up being the middleman, basically documenting what Marc took and reporting back to Bruce. Then Classic Auctions and Bruce teamed up to get the Al Ruelle photo collection—he'd been a famous photographer in Boston. Because I wasn't working, they asked me if I wanted to scan the collection. I had no idea what I was getting into. It was a huge undertaking, and it took me almost a year to scan the entire thing. From there, there were other collections to scan, and I ended up an employee. Now I'm the shipper, scanner, delivery man and the guy who picks people up people at airport. I'm the MVP here—the Most Valuable Pooch.

It's kind of a karmic thing. I fucking hated hockey and I didn't want anything to do with it, and now it's in my face 24 hours a day. The current Montreal Canadiens come around pretty regularly, and tickets get offered here and there, but I just don't care.

It is a kick seeing some of my old colleagues, though. I helped broker a deal for Mike Amodeo to sell some of his relics, but when Marc asked me to call other friends from my past, I found I just couldn't do it; it felt too weird—"Hey, how you doing? Got anything to sell?"

There's that weird "What if?" when I talk to some of them, too. Mike was my best friend, but we didn't stay in touch. He ended up as a salesman for Moosehead beer. Yet the couple of times we talked on the phone as I was writing this book, it felt like we'd seen each other yesterday. Probably more than anyone, he has a good sense of what could have been for me.

> **MIKE AMODEO:** It's apropos. He did it his way. He had the opportunity. Long and short, he had all the tools, there's no two ways about it. When Gilley concentrated, my goodness, no one better . . . Things came natural to Gilley, like everything he touched was gold forever. For us normal guys . . . There are people out there that are blessed that way. My blessing was the fact that I stayed employed all those years.

Guys from my era, like Marcel Dionne or Guy Lapointe, come by Classic Auctions sometimes. We chit-chat, though I think I'm pretty oblivious to it all. Billy Smith, the legendary Islanders goalie, was here, and someone brought him by to say hello. I was busy and didn't really look up, just shaking his hand and continuing to work. It was rude. A few minutes later, someone else said, "Billy Smith is here." Huh? I went upstairs and asked someone else, and she said, "You just shook his hand." So I went down and reintroduced myself to Billy, and apologized for being rude. I told him that I probably smoked too much pot in my life.

Classic Auctions always has a big booth at the Sportcard & Memorabilia Expo in Toronto, up by the airport. I went for a number of years, but eventually it would just kill my back. It was strange, reconnecting with unexpected people from my past, like Dave Lively, the guy who used to go get me hot dogs during games when I was the backup goalie with the Toros.

One time, Marc and I went to pick up Bobby Hull, who was staying at a friend's place. Marc had bought his collection at one point. I knocked on the door, and Bobby came out. He's got no hair, and he looks like he's 83. He looks at me and he doesn't recognize me. I say, "Hi, Bobby" and he keeps looking at me. "Who are you?" Finally, I say who I am. "Oh, yeah! I remember." We then went to the hotel and had lunch with Bobby and his son Brett, who had to help him up and down the stairs, since he could hardly walk.

I fucked with hockey in a way—I didn't put much into the game, and I got a lot of money out of it. Right now, I'm not getting much money, but I'm putting a lot in. Funny, isn't it? It's kind of backwards—but somehow it also makes sense.

ACKNOWLEDGEMENTS

GILLES GRATTON

I want to thank Greg for listening to my stories and making it all make sense, and his wife and son for accommodating me when I came to visit. And it's Bruce Jessop that deserves all the credit for pushing me to do the book and connecting me with Greg. Bruce had suggested over the years that I write my autobiography, but I always said no; now, with two kids almost ready for university, the extra income will be most welcome!

Mike Amodeo, my partner in crime, always made me laugh and was first-hand witness to most of my craziness. In Ottawa and Toronto, Tom Martin was a great influence as well, sort of an anti–Mike Amodeo, and Gavin Kirk and Pat Hickey deserve thank-yous as well.

I can't forget the Dillon family, who were so great to me; there's my musical collaborator Brian, my ball hockey buddies Wayne and Gary, Mom Dillon for the great food, and Papa Dillon, who tried to counsel me through my struggles.

My two buddies in New York, Rod Gilbert and Mike McEwen, both stepped up to share stories of our time together.

Rod truly made my year with the Rangers bearable, and he took care of me in so many ways. McEwen was a good roommate and liked many of the same recreational pursuits that I did.

My family has been supportive through the process, especially Karine, Claudine, François and Chantal. Claude Bertrand has been a pal for 60 years and proved it here, and my travelling buddy Pierre Gagne clocks in at 40 years of friendship, including trips to Russia, Spain and the Bahamas.

Finally, I want to thank Dan Bouchard, who made all this possible. He encouraged and pushed me to keep playing. He is the reason I had a hockey career at all.

GREG OLIVER

One of my favourite sports books of all time is Terry Pluto's *Loose Balls*, which is essentially a collection of quotes from players and management of the old American Basketball Association, pieced together to tell the history of the upstart league. This book, with so many other voices coming in and out of the narrative, owes a debt to Pluto. Another model was the autobiography of John Lydon of the Sex Pistols, *Rotten*, which also brings in contemporaries to better explain both Johnny Rotten and his times.

It was Bruce Jessop who thought I'd be a good fit for working with Gilles on his life story, and I think he was right. When Bruce read a portion of the manuscript and said it sounded like Gilles, I knew I was on the right track. Thanks to Michael Holmes, my editor, for steering the process after saying yes.

Having heard many of the stories about Gilles, it was a surprise to host a polite, calm, friendly house guest for a weekend to get the book rolling. Naturally, that leads to a thank you to my wife, Meredith, and son, Quinn, not only for letting a stranger bunk in the house—on Meredith's birthday weekend, no less—but also for their love and support.

My writing partner on *Don't Call Me Goon* and *The Goaltenders' Union*, Richard Kamchen, was privy to much of the project, and offered valuable, honest thoughts along the way—he doesn't know how to pull his punches, which is both a pro and a con!

Then there's a host of others who helped in some way or another: Lance Hornby; Oshawa Generals historian Wayne Kewin; Steve Williamson; the staff at the Hockey Hall of Fame's D.K. (Doc) Seaman Hockey Resource Centre (especially Craig, Miragh and Katherine); the folks behind the Toros reunion in the summer of 2015 (Paul, Mike, Tom, John); Stewart Henderson and the Mask Fest fanatics; and my friends at the Society for International Hockey Research who encouraged me at various meetings, especially fellow authors Kevin Shea, Eric Zweig and Todd Denault.

SELECTED BIBLIOGRAPHY

The Big M: The Frank Mahovlich Story, by Ted Mahovlich, HarperCollins, Toronto, 1999.

The Goaltenders Union: Hockey's Greatest Puckstoppers, Acrobats, and Flakes, by Greg Oliver and Richard Kamchen, ECW Press, Toronto, 2014.

Hockey Hall of Fame Book of Goalies: Profiles, Memorabilia, Essays and Stats, edited by Steve Cameron, Firefly Books, Richmond Hill, ON, 2010.

In the Crease: Goaltenders Look at Life in the NHL, by Dick Irvin, McClelland & Stewart, Toronto, 1995.

Left Wing and a Prayer: Birth Pains of a World Hockey Franchise, by Doug Michel, as told to Bob Mellor, Excalibur, 1974.

The New York Rangers: Broadway's Longest Running Hit, by John Kreiser and Lou Freidman, Sports Publishing, Inc., 1997.

The Rebel League: The Short and Unruly Life of the World Hockey Association, by Ed Willes, McClelland & Stewart, Toronto, 2004.

Saving Face: The Art and History of the Goalie Mask, by Jim Hynes and Gary Smith, Wiley, Mississauga, ON, 2008.

INTERVIEWS

Allen Abel

Mike Amodeo

Claude Bertrand

Les Binkley

Mike Boland

Dan Bouchard

Bob Charlebois

Frederic Cloutier

Claudine Cloutier-Gratton

Steve Cuddie

John Davidson

Brian Dillon

Pierre Gagne

Rod Gilbert

François Gratton

Karine Gratton

Billy Harris

Greg Harrison

Pat Hickey

Mark Howe

Jeff Jacques

Bruce Jessop

Doug Keeler

Bob Kelly

Wayne Kewin

Gavin Kirk

David Lively

Bill Lochead

Roy MacGregor

Tom Martin

Pete McAskile

Ted McComb

Mike McEwen

Chantal Puyleart

Nelson Pyatt

Rick Sentes

Jim Shaw

Peter Sullivan

Dave Tataryn

STATISTICS

SEASON	TEAM	LEAGUE	NO	GP	W	L	T	MIN	GA	SO	GAA	PIM
1968–69	LaSalle	GOJBHL		Statistics not available								
1969–70	Oshawa Generals	OHA-Jr. A	1	28	8	15	3	1561	129	0	4.96	10
	Playoffs			3	0	3	0	160	15	0	5.62	4
1970–71	Oshawa Generals	OHA-Jr. A	30	52	15	28	4	2871	239	0	4.99	40
1971–72	Oshawa Generals	OHA-Jr. A	30	55	30	13	8	2980	182	1	3.66	24
	Playoffs			11	5	5	1	660	35	0	3.18	2
1972–73	Ottawa Nationals	WHA	33	51	25	22	3	3021	187	0	3.71	10
	Playoffs			2	0	1	0	87	7	0	4.83	0
1973–74	Toronto Toros	WHA	33	57	26	24	3	3200	188	2	3.53	28
	Playoffs			10	5	3	0	539	25	1	2.78	5
	WHA All Stars (East)	WHA	33	Statistics not available								
1974–75	Toronto Toros	WHA	33	53	30	20	1	2881	185	2	3.85	8
	Team Canada		33	2	–	–	–	55	1	–	–	2
	Playoffs			1	0	1	0	36	5	0	8.33	0
1975–76	St. Louis Blues	NHL	33	6	2	0	2	265	11	0	2.49	2
1976–77	New York Rangers	NHL	33	41	11	18	7	2034	143	0	4.22	13
1977–78	New Haven Nighthawks	AHL	34	1	0	1	0	60	6	0	6.00	0
Season Totals				344	147	141	31	18873	1270	5		135
Playoff Totals				27	10	13	1	1482	87	1		11
NHL Season Totals				47	13	18	9	2299	154	0		15

No.: jersey number
GP: games played
W/L/T: wins/losses ties
Min: minutes played

GA: goals against
SO: shutouts
GAA: goals-against average
PIM: penalties in minutes

Courtesy Society for International Hockey Research

ALSO BY GREG OLIVER

Father Bauer and the Great Experiment:
The Genesis of Canadian Olympic Hockey

Blue Lines, Goal Lines & Bottom Lines: Hockey Contracts and
Historical Documents from the Collection of Allan Stitt

Written in Blue & White: The Toronto Maple Leafs Contracts
and Historical Documents from the Collection of Allan Stitt

The Goaltenders' Union: Hockey's Greatest Puckstoppers,
Acrobats, and Flakes (with Richard Kamchen)

Don't Call Me Goon: Hockey's Greatest Enforcers, Gunslingers,
and Bad Boys (with Richard Kamchen)

Duck with the Puck (with Quinn Oliver)

SLAM! Wrestling: Shocking Stories from the Squared
Circle (Editor, with Jon Waldman)

The Pro Wrestling Hall of Fame: Heroes & Icons (with Steven Johnson)

The Pro Wrestling Hall of Fame: The Heels (with Steven Johnson)

The Pro Wrestling Hall of Fame: The Tag Teams (with Steven Johnson)

The Pro Wrestling Hall of Fame: The Canadians

Benoit: Wrestling with the Horror That Destroyed a Family and Crippled
a Sport (with Steven Johnson, Irv Muchnick and Heath McCoy)

GILLES GRATTON is a former goaltender who currently works with Classic Auctions, a historical hockey memorabilia auction house. He lives in Montreal with his wife, Anne, and teenaged children, William and Charlotte. For more on Gilles, visit his website, gillesgratton.com.

GREG OLIVER is the author of numerous books and has contributed to a wide range of publications, from the *Hockey News* to *Scouting Life* to the *Globe and Mail*. He lives in Toronto with his wife, Meredith, and son, Quinn. Follow him on Twitter @gregmep and visit his website, oliverbooks.ca.